Vicki Anderson with Eoin Higgins,
Cristina Rusu, Diana Todoran
and Ioana Tudose

**Limba modernă 1 –
studiu intensiv**

Engleză

Caietul elevului

Clasa a VI-a

6

CAMBRIDGE

Prezentul auxiliar a fost avizat de Ministerul Educației și Cercetării prin Ordinul nr. 5318 din 21.11.2019 și se regăsește la poziția nr. 38 din anexa Ordinului.

Prezentul auxiliar este în conformitate cu Programa școlară pentru disciplina *Limba modernă 1 – studiu intensiv. Clasele a V-a – a VIII-a*, aprobată prin ordinul ministrului nr. 3393/2017.

Această lucrare însoţeşte manualul Editurii Art Klett, *Limba modernă 1 – studiu intensiv. Engleză. Clasa a VI-a*, realizat în coeditare cu Cambridge University Press, autori: Ben Goldstein, Ceri Jones, Emma Heyderman, Cristina Rusu, Diana Todoran, Ioana Tudose.

Coordonator redacție: Cătălin Georgescu
Editor-coordonator: Gabriela Pérez Ortíz
Redactare: John Ryan, Ioana Tudose, Elena Chiruță
Corectură: Helen Lumb, David Richardson
Tehnoredactare: Anca Vrănescu, Valentina Dobrescu
Copertă: Florin Paraschiv

Înregistrări și procesare sunet: Ian Harker, Dave Morritt, BraveArts, ML Sistems Consulting;
voci: Helen Lumb, David Richardson
Pistele audio ale exercițiilor de tip *Listening* pot fi ascultate și descărcate la următoarea adresă:

Descrierea CIP a Bibliotecii Naţionale a României
Limba modernă 1: Engleză – studiu intensiv: caietul elevului: clasa a VI-a /
Vicki Anderson with Eoin Higgins, Cristina Rusu, ... – București: Art Klett, 2024
ISBN 978-606-076-869-2
I. Anderson, Vicki
II. Higgins, Eoin
III. Rusu, Cristina
811.111

Această publicaţie este înregistrată la British Library.
ISBN 978-100-981-384-6

Lucrarea este rezultatul colaborării dintre Cambridge University Press și Editura Art Klett.
Prelucrare după **Eyes Open Level 2, Workbook**, Vicki Anderson with Eoin Higgins and **Eyes Open Level 3, Workbook**, Vicki Anderson with Eoin Higgins © Cambridge University Press 2015, în parteneriat cu Discovery Education™

Editura Art Klett
C.P. 12, O.P. 63, cod 014880, sector 1, București
Telefoane: 021 796 73 83, (021) 796 73 80; fax: (021) 369 31 99
Comenzi online: www.art-educational.ro

Foreword

Cambridge uses cutting-edge language and pedagogy research to create innovative materials that teachers and students will love.

English and Romanian teachers have created, through *Limba modernă 1 – studiu intensiv. Engleză. Clasa a VI-a*, **a textbook that follows the Romanian Curriculum step by step.**

With *Limba modernă 1 – studiu intensiv. Engleză. Clasa a VI-a,* **learning English becomes much more interesting as you discover and explore the cultures and people of the world around you.**

The Workbook for *Limba modernă 1 – studiu intensiv. Engleză. Clasa a VI-a* **offers additional practice of all the language and skills presented in the Student's Book through:**

- **graded exercises for mixed abilities;**
- **more help with grammar and speaking in** *Speaking extra* **and** *Language focus extra* **pages;**
- **Cambridge Learner Corpus informed** *Get it Right!* **pages.**

Contents

Starter Unit page 5

1 Money matters page 11

2 Our heroes page 23

3 At home page 35

4 A balancing act page 47

5 Visions of the future page 59

6 Life choices page 71

7 Look out! page 83

8 Having fun! page 95

9 Reading for pleasure page 107

Speaking extra page 113

Language focus extra page 123

Starter Unit

General and specific competences from the curriculum explored in the unit

1. Understand oral messages in different communication situations
1.1. Identify essential information from the news presented on TV/recorded materials related to different events, when the comment is illustrated by pictures
1.2. Identify details from messages and interactions on predictable topics, when the speakers/interlocutors talk clearly and slowly
1.3. Identify specific aspects of the culture of the language studied

2. Speak in different communication situations
2.1. Present plans, intentions and future projects
2.2. Give a short and simple presentation on activities
2.3. Initiate, continue and finish a dialogue on familiar or personal interest topics
2.4. Participate in conversations related to planning activities
2.5. Show interest in participating in a verbal exchange

3. Understand written messages in different communication situations
3.1. Select necessary information from lists or simple functional texts (brochures, menus, schedules, ads)
3.2. Extract information from multiple short texts based on several predefined or negotiated criteria/constraints
3.3. Identify information from a simple written letter/email to write an answer
3.4. Show willingness to be informed through reading

4. Write messages in everyday communication situations
4.1. Complete a form with personally identifiable information (education, interests, competences)
4.2. Write a very simple personal letter (digital version included) to express thanks or apologies
4.3. Tell a story, in short, using linkers to emphasise the chronological order
4.4. Write simple and coherent texts on specific topics of interest
4.5. Participate in the exchange of written messages

Competenţele generale şi specifice din programa şcolară, urmărite în unitatea de învăţare

1. Receptarea de mesaje orale în diverse situaţii de comunicare
1.1. Identificarea informaţiilor esenţiale din ştirile prezentate la TV/materiale înregistrate, referitoare la diferite evenimente, atunci când comentariul este ilustrat prin imagini
1.2. Identificarea detaliilor din mesaje și interacţiuni pe subiecte previzibile când locutorii/interlocutorii vorbesc clar și rar
1.3. Identificarea unor elemente culturale specifice limbii studiate

2. Exprimarea orală în diverse situaţii de comunicare
2.1. Prezentarea unor planuri/unor intenţii și proiecte de viitor
2.2. Descrierea scurtă, elementară a unor activități
2.3. Inițierea, susținerea și încheierea unui dialog pe teme familiare sau de interes personal
2.4. Participarea la conversaţii în legătură cu planificarea unor activităţi
2.5. Manifestarea interesului pentru participarea la schimbul verbal

3. Receptarea de mesaje scrise în diverse situaţii de comunicare
3.1. Extragerea informaţiilor necesare din liste sau din texte funcţionale simple (pliante, meniuri, orare, reclame)
3.2. Extragerea informațiilor din mai multe texte scurte pe baza mai multor criterii/constrângeri prestabilite sau negociate
3.3. Identificarea informaţiilor dintr-o scrisoare personală simplă/e-mail în vederea redactării unui răspuns
3.4. Manifestarea disponibilităţii pentru informare prin lectură

4. Redactarea de mesaje în diverse situaţii de comunicare
4.1. Completarea unui formular cu informaţii de identificare (educaţie, interese, competenţe)
4.2. Redactarea unei scrisori personale (inclusiv digitale) foarte simple exprimând mulțumiri sau scuze
4.3. Relatarea pe scurt a unei întâmplări utilizând cuvinte de legătură pentru a marca ordinea cronologică
4.4. Redactarea de texte simple și coerente pe teme de interes
4.5. Participarea la schimbul de mesaje scrise

Starter Unit

Family

1 ★ Put the letters in order to make family words.

1 umm _mum_
2 dda ______
3 madrang ______
4 enrpast ______
5 leunc ______
6 rtborhe ______
7 fewi ______
8 trisse ______
9 natu ______
10 sicuno ______
11 dradngad ______
12 baunsdh ______

2 ★★ Match the words in Exercise 1 to make pairs.

1 wife – _husband_
2 uncle – ______
3 grandma – ______
4 dad – ______
5 brother – ______

3 ★★★ Complete the definitions.

1 My mum and dad are my _parents_.
2 My aunt's husband is my ______.
3 My granddad's wife is my ______.
4 My aunt's children are my ______.
5 My grandma and granddad are my ______.
6 My dad's wife is my ______.
7 My mum and dad's child is my ______ or ______.

Subject pronouns and *be*

4 ★ Circle the correct options.

1 Where am (I) / you?
2 **Is / Are** you from Canada?
3 Daniel **am / is** my cousin. **He / They** is 14.
4 My sister's birthday **are / is** in May.
5 My grandparents **are / is** in Japan. **She's / They're** on holiday.
6 My brother and I **am / are** at the zoo. **We / They** are not at school.
7 I **am / is** at the cinema. Are **you / he** at the shops?

be

5 ★★ Complete the sentences and questions with the correct form of *be*.

1 _Are_ you at home?
2 This ______ my mum.
3 We ______ best friends.
4 ______ they from England?
5 His sister ______ in my class.
6 I ______ from Edinburgh, Scotland.
7 ______ you on the school football team?
8 My new dog ______ called Bob.

Possessive *'s*

6 ★ Complete the sentences with *'s* in the correct place.

1 My mum ^'s car is red.
2 Our cousin house is in the city.
3 Is this your granddad piano?
4 What's your dad name?
5 My best friend birthday is in October.
6 His sister dance classes are on Monday.
7 Is our dog nose brown?
8 Where is my brother T-shirt?

Starter Unit

School subjects

1 ★★ **Look at the pictures and complete the crossword with the school subjects.**

down

across

2 ★★ **Match the school subjects with the sentences.**

ICT	Geography	French	~~History~~	
Maths	PE	Science	English	Music

1 'Let's talk about the year 1914.' *History*
2 'What does *je m'appelle* mean?' ______
3 'OK, run around the gym ten times.' ______
4 'Turn on the computers, please.' ______
5 'Let's play it again and listen to the piano.' ______
6 'Water is hydrogen and … what else?' ______
7 'What is 15 x 147?' ______
8 'Where are the Rocky Mountains?' ______
9 'Let's look at the verb *to be*.' ______

there is/are + some and any

3 ★★ **Find five more differences between Picture A and Picture B and write them down. Use *there is*(*n't*) / *there are*(*n't*).**

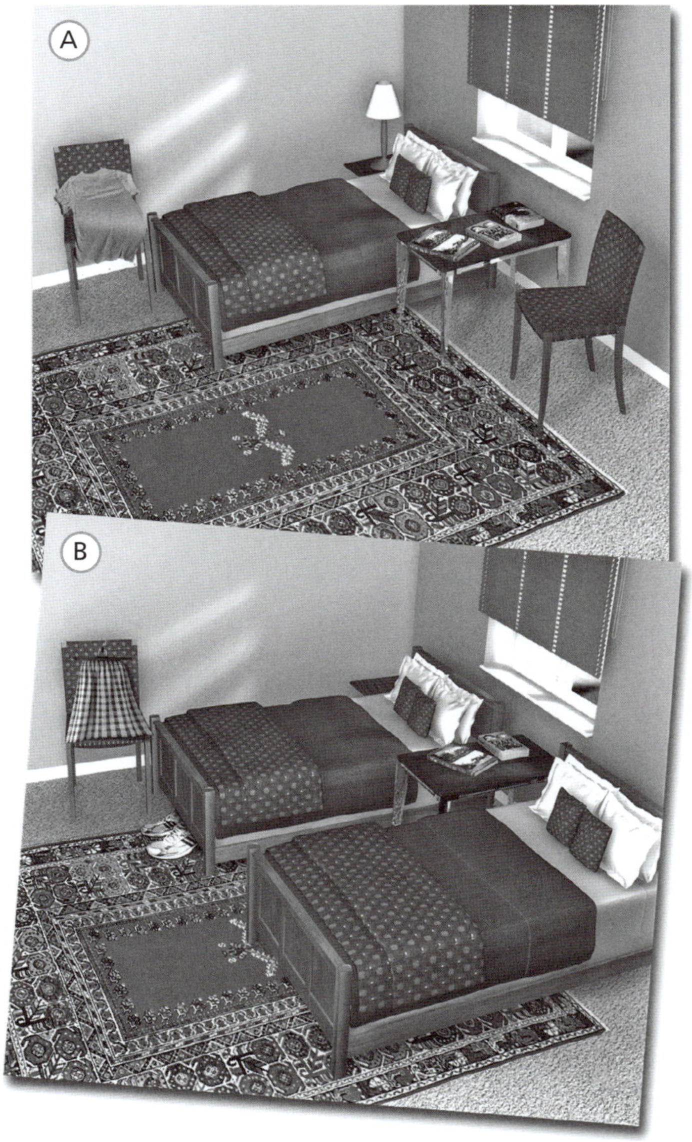

1 *In Picture A there are three books. In Picture B there are two.*
2 ______
3 ______
4 ______
5 ______
6 ______

Starter Unit

UNIT S

1 ★★ **Circle the correct options and complete the sentences with *some* or *any*.**

1 There isn't / aren't ___any___ cheese in the fridge.
2 Are / Is there __________ giraffes in the zoo?
3 Is there / Are there __________ T-shirts in your bag?
4 There is / are __________ fruit in the kitchen.
5 There isn't / aren't __________ boats on the river.
6 Is there / Are there __________ pasta in the cupboard?
7 There is / are __________ good photos on your mobile phone.
8 There isn't / aren't __________ money in my bag.

have got

2 ★ **Circle the correct options.**

1 I've / 's got a new computer.
2 **Have / Has** you got a mobile phone?
3 My sister **have / has** got a TV in her room.
4 We **'ve / 's** got a pet cat. His name is Peru.
5 **Have / Has** he got your phone number?
6 They **'ve / 's** got two houses in the city.
7 She **haven't / hasn't** got a brother.
8 Our dog **'ve / 's** got a tennis ball.
9 We **haven't / hasn't** got a big family.

Sports and activities

3 ★★ **Put the letters in order to make sports and activities. Then complete the sentences with the correct form of *play*, *do* or *go*.**

1 Do you ___play___ ___basketball___ at your school? (sblaltabke)
2 I'd like to __________ __________ in the evenings. (gyoa)
3 We __________ __________ in the mountains every winter. (gisnki)
4 Can you __________ __________? (yalolblelv)
5 My brother __________ __________ every Saturday. (duoj)
6 A lot of people __________ __________ in the sea in Ireland. (fnruisg)
7 My family sometimes __________ __________ in the lake. (mgnswmii)
8 Let's __________ __________ at the skatepark later. (aasgbtdkineor)
9 Do you often __________ __________ with your friends? (libogwn)
10 I want to __________ __________, but my brother's got my bike. (liccgyn)

Present simple: affirmative and negative

4 ★ **Circle the correct words in the grammar table.**

1	I/You/We/They **watch / watches** TV.
2	He/She/It **finish / finishes** at five.
3	We **don't / doesn't** like carrots.
4	She **don't / doesn't** like bananas.

5 ★★ **Complete the text with the present simple form of the verbs in brackets.**

My family [1] ___loves___ (love) sport. We all [2] __________ (play) one sport or more. My dad [3] __________ (play) tennis every Saturday. My mum [4] __________ (go) to the gym and [5] __________ (do) yoga twice a week. I [6] __________ (do) karate after school and every weekend I [7] __________ (go) skateboarding with friends. My brother [8] __________ (play) basketball and he [9] __________ (train) four days a week. We often [10] __________ (go) to see him play. We [11] __________ (not watch) sport on TV because we [12] __________ (not like) watching TV.

Starter Unit

Present simple: *Yes/No* questions

1 ★ **Circle the correct words in the grammar table.**

1	**Do you / You** like karate?
2	Yes, I **do / does**. No, I **don't / doesn't**.
3	**He / Does he** play tennis?
4	Yes, he **do / does**. No, he **don't / doesn't**.

2 ★★ **Complete the questions and answers with the correct form of *do*.**

1 *Do* you do your homework in the evening? Yes, I *do*.
2 ________ Harry and Gina go cycling on Saturdays? No, they ________.
3 ________ Nina like Geography? No, she ________.
4 ________ your friends go skateboarding? Yes, they ________.
5 ________ they use the internet to study French? No, they ________.
6 ________ your brother do karate? Yes, he ________.
7 ________ your teacher show videos in English class? No, she ________.

Present simple: *Wh-* questions

3 ★★ **Match the question words with the words in the box.**

person object/thing place ~~frequency~~ time reason

1 how often *frequency*
2 what ________
3 when ________
4 where ________
5 who ________
6 why ________

4 ★★ **Complete the questions with the correct question word from the box.**

How often What When ~~Where~~ Who Why Where

1 A: *Where do you live?* (you / live)
B: In London.
2 A: ________ does he study?
B: English and Maths.
3 A: ________ do they play sports?
B: Once a week.
4 A: ________ does he go cycling with?
B: His brother.
5 A: ________ do you like skateboarding?
B: Because it's fun.
6 A: ________ does she play volleyball?
B: In the park.
7 A: ________ does he go to drama class?
B: On Saturdays.

Adverbs of frequency

5 ★ **Circle the correct words in the grammar table.**

1	Going swimming with my friends **is always / always is** good fun.
2	We **go sometimes / sometimes go** to the sports centre on Saturdays.

6 ★★ **Put the words in the correct order to make sentences.**

1 football / play / school / at / We / always
We always play football at school.
2 Football / sometimes / matches / long / are / very
____
3 never / me / with / My dad / chess / plays
____
4 We / often / Saturdays / on / go / cycling
____
5 dictionaries / use / English class / usually / We / in
____
6 are / His / really interesting / books / always
____

1 Money matters

General and specific competences from the curriculum explored in the unit

1. Understand oral messages in different communication situations
1.1. Identify essential information from the news presented on TV/recorded materials related to different events, when the comment is illustrated by pictures
1.2. Identify details from messages and interactions on predictable topics, when the speakers/interlocutors talk clearly and slowly
1.3. Identify specific aspects of the culture of the language studied

2. Speak in different communication situations
2.1. Present plans, intentions and future projects
2.2. Give a short and simple presentation on activities
2.3. Initiate, continue and finish a dialogue on familiar or personal interest topics
2.4. Participate in conversations related to planning activities
2.5. Show interest in participating in a verbal exchange

3. Understand written messages in different communication situations
3.1. Select necessary information from lists or simple functional texts (brochures, menus, schedules, ads)
3.2. Extract information from multiple short texts based on several predefined or negotiated criteria/constraints
3.3. Identify information from a simple written letter/email to write an answer
3.4. Show willingness to be informed through reading

4. Write messages in everyday communication situations
4.1. Complete a form with personally identifiable information (education, interests, competences)
4.2. Write a very simple personal letter (digital version included) to express thanks or apologies
4.3. Tell a story, in short, using linkers to emphasise the chronological order
4.4. Write simple and coherent texts on specific topics of interest
4.5. Participate in the exchange of written messages

Competenţele generale şi specifice din programa şcolară, urmărite în unitatea de învăţare

1. Receptarea de mesaje orale în diverse situaţii de comunicare
1.1. Identificarea informaţiilor esenţiale din ştirile prezentate la TV/materiale înregistrate, referitoare la diferite evenimente, atunci când comentariul este ilustrat prin imagini
1.2. Identificarea detaliilor din mesaje şi interacţiuni pe subiecte previzibile când locutorii/interlocutorii vorbesc clar şi rar
1.3. Identificarea unor elemente culturale specifice limbii studiate

2. Exprimarea orală în diverse situaţii de comunicare
2.1. Prezentarea unor planuri/unor intenţii şi proiecte de viitor
2.2. Descrierea scurtă, elementară a unor activităţi
2.3. Iniţierea, susţinerea şi încheierea unui dialog pe teme familiare sau de interes personal
2.4. Participarea la conversaţii în legătură cu planificarea unor activităţi
2.5. Manifestarea interesului pentru participarea la schimbul verbal

3. Receptarea de mesaje scrise în diverse situaţii de comunicare
3.1. Extragerea informaţiilor necesare din liste sau din texte funcţionale simple (pliante, meniuri, orare, reclame)
3.2. Extragerea informaţiilor din mai multe texte scurte pe baza mai multor criterii/constrângeri prestabilite sau negociate
3.3. Identificarea informaţiilor dintr-o scrisoare personală simplă/e-mail în vederea redactării unui răspuns
3.4. Manifestarea disponibilităţii pentru informare prin lectură

4. Redactarea de mesaje în diverse situaţii de comunicare
4.1. Completarea unui formular cu informaţii de identificare (educaţie, interese, competenţe)
4.2. Redactarea unei scrisori personale (inclusiv digitale) foarte simple exprimând mulţumiri sau scuze
4.3. Relatarea pe scurt a unei întâmplări utilizând cuvinte de legătură pentru a marca ordinea cronologică
4.4. Redactarea de texte simple şi coerente pe teme de interes
4.5. Participarea la schimbul de mesaje scrise

1 Money matters

Vocabulary

Shops

1 ★ Find ten shops in the word search.

e	l	s	p	o	r	t	s	o	c	d
l	c	v	e	n	m	o	s	o	h	e
e	p	r	d	z	u	s	h	y	e	p
c	b	m	t	h	s	x	o	o	m	a
t	g	l	d	e	i	n	e	u	i	r
r	q	j	b	d	c	t	e	r	s	t
o	b	o	o	k	s	h	o	p	t	m
n	p	l	c	e	u	w	z	m	e	e
i	v	c	l	o	t	h	e	s	t	n
c	n	e	i	l	r	m	e	r	p	t
s	u	p	e	r	m	a	r	k	e	t
s	n	e	w	s	a	g	e	n	t	b

2 ★ Complete the table with the words from Exercise 1.

1 Five words that go with *shop*	
sports shop	________ shop
________ shop	________ shop
________ shop	
2 One word that goes with *store*	
________ store	
3 Four words that are ONE word	
________	________
________	________

3 ★★ Complete the sentences with words from Exercise 1.

1 You can buy trainers and boots in a *shoe shop*.
2 I need some aspirin from the ________.
3 My favourite shop is the ________ because it sells magazines and chocolate.
4 I like that ________ because it's got great T-shirts and cheap jeans.
5 I'd like to look at some laptops – let's go to the ________.
6 Why don't you go to the ________ to buy a book for your dad's birthday?
7 We're going to the ________ to buy fruit, vegetables and some other things.
8 I like the guitars in this ________.

4 ★★ Complete the text with words from Exercise 1.

There is a shopping centre in my town, but my friends and I don't often go there. It's got a [1] *newsagent* where you can buy magazines or birthday cards, and a couple of [2] ________ with jeans and T-shirts, but nothing cool for teenagers. My mum and dad love the [3] ________ because you can find everything you need there. There are some shops I like. There's a [4] ________ with great trainers, and there's also an [5] ________ with lots of tablets and smartphones, but they're a bit expensive. My favourite is the [6] ________ because it plays all the new songs, and a lot of young people go there.

5 ★★★ Write about a shopping centre you know. Complete the sentences about it.

1 It's got a *big department store*.
2 There's a ________ where you can buy ________ and ________.
3 I like the ________ because it's got ________.
4 I don't go to the ________ because it hasn't got ________.
5 My mum and dad like the ________ because ________.

Language focus 1

Present continuous

1 ★ **Circle the correct words in the grammar table.**

1	She's looking / looking at boots in the shoe shop.
2	They **not buying / aren't buying** those T-shirts.
3	**Are you coming / You are coming** with us?
4	Yes, **I'm / I am**. No, we **aren't / isn't**.
5	To talk about facts, habits and routines, use the present **simple / continuous**.
6	To talk about an action in progress, use the present **simple / continuous**.

2 ★★ **Complete the conversations with the present continuous form of the verbs in brackets.**

Joe: Hi Bob. We[1] *'re meeting* (meet) outside the shopping centre. Where are you?
Bob: I [2] ____________ (sit) on the bus. Where are you?
Joe: Outside the shopping centre. Ian and I [3] ____________ (wait) for you now.
Bob: OK. There's a lot of traffic. The bus [4] ____________ (not go) very fast.
Joe: Well, we [5] ____________ (not stay) here for a long time. It's cold! Where's the bus now?
Bob: It [6] ____________ (come) into Mill Street, so see you in two minutes.

3 ★★ **Complete the questions and short answers with the correct form of the present continuous. Use the words in the box.**

you sell	we have	~~he look~~
you spend	they buy	Lisa wait

1 *Is he looking for a book in English?*
Yes, he is.
2 ____________________ your old video games?
Yes, ____________, for £5 each.
3 ________________________________ that CD?
No, ____________.
4 ______________________________ lunch now?
No, ____________, just a drink.
5 ______________________________ in the café?
No, ____________. She's late.
6 ___________________________ £20 on a T-shirt?
Yes, ____________. It's a present.

Present simple vs. continuous

4 ★★ **Circle the correct words in the text.**

My sister and I [1]**try / are trying** an experiment at the moment – no shopping for a month! Usually Mum [2]**gives / is giving** me pocket money on Saturday and my friends and I [3]**go / are going** shopping in the afternoon, but this Saturday is different. My friends [4]**shop / are shopping** for clothes and things, but I [5]**write / 'm writing** this blog at home. Why? Well, I [6]**have / am having** a lot of things that I never [7]**wear / am wearing**. This month my sister Jane and I [8]**put / are putting** our pocket money in our money boxes for our holidays, and we [9]**do / are doing** lots of other things. Shopping all the time is boring!

5 ★★★ **Write the questions in the present simple or present continuous and answer them for you.**

1 What / wear / at the moment?
What are you wearing at the moment?
I'm wearing ...
2 you / reading / a good book / at the moment?
____
____
3 Where / usually / buy your clothes?
____
____
4 What / at the weekend / get up / time / you?
____
____
5 you / music / What / listen to?
____
____
6 When / next year / start / school?
____
____

Explore extreme adjectives

6 ★★ **Complete the definitions with the adjectives in the box.**

huge	~~great~~	wonderful	amazing
brilliant	boiling	awful	freezing

1 When something is very good we say it's *great*, ____________, ____________ or ____________.
2 When it's very hot, we say it's ____________.
3 When something is very big, we say it's ____________.
4 When it's very cold, we say it's ____________.
5 When something is very bad, we say it's ____________.

Listening and vocabulary

Money verbs

1 ★ **Match the verbs in the box with the correct definition.**

sell	spend	save	~~earn~~	buy	borrow

1 get money from working *earn*
2 get money from someone to keep for a short time ______
3 what a shop does ______
4 pay money to get something specific ______
5 use money for something, not only in shops ______
6 keep money so you can use it in the future ______

2 ★★ **Complete the sentences with the verbs from Exercise 1.**

1 I'm trying to *save* my pocket money for a new smartphone.
2 Jane wants to ______ all her video games for £10 each.
3 Can I ______ £5 from you until tomorrow?
4 Some people ______ a lot of money on clothes.
5 How much money does a shop assistant ______?
6 I want to ______ some new skates this year.

3 ★★★ **Write the answers to the questions. Use the present continuous and the words in brackets.**

1 What are you doing on eBay? (sell / my computer)
I'm selling my computer.
2 Why are you putting money in that box? (save for / new bike)
______
3 Why are you going to Helen's house? (borrow / her dress)
______
4 Why are you in the sports shop? (buy / new trainers)
______
5 What are you doing? (spend / five pounds / sweets)
______
6 Why are you cleaning your dad's car? (earn / money / a new phone)
______

Listening

4 ★ ***Listen to the conversation between Gemma and her mum. What is Gemma's problem? Circle the correct option.**

a clothes b money c her brother

5 ★★ **Read the sentences. Listen again and circle the correct options.**

1 Gemma wants to buy a pair of jeans **online** / **at the shopping centre**.
2 Gemma's pocket money is **£50** / **£30** a month.
3 **Gemma** / **Gemma's brother** saves money.
4 Gemma says she needs more money than her brother because **she's older** / **he only buys video games**.
5 The cinema costs **£5** / **£10**.
6 Her mum tells Gemma to **do work in their house** / **get a babysitting job**.
7 Gemma **likes** / **doesn't like** her mum's idea.
8 Gemma's mum gives her **more money** / **a job**.

* Pistele audio ale exercițiilor pot fi ascultate și descărcate la următoarea adresă:

Language focus 2

(don't) want to, would(n't) like to, would prefer to, would rather/ would sooner

1 ★ **Circle the correct options.**

1 Would / Do you like to save more money?
2 Would you **prefer / want** the black T-shirt or the white one?
3 I'd **want / like** to go to the electronics shop to see some new mobile phones.
4 She **doesn't want / wouldn't prefer** to borrow money from her sister.
5 Would you **like / want** to go to the bookshop?
6 I **wouldn't like / don't prefer** to buy a new car.
7 Dad wants to have dinner at 8, but I'd rather **to have / have** dinner at 7.
8 Sebi doesn't really want to go back to Bulgaria this year. He'd sooner **go / going** to Greece.

2 ★ **Match the questions with the answers.**

1 Does your friend want to come with us? *c*
2 Would you like to listen to music? ___
3 Would Barry prefer to go to the sports shop? ___
4 Do they want to invite Paul to come shopping? ___
5 Would Mary and Arthur like to go to a café? ___
6 Would Claudia prefer to do the exam today? ___

a Yes, he would.
b No, they wouldn't.
c No, she doesn't.
d Yes, she would.
e Yes, I would.
f Yes, they do.

3 ★★ **Complete the sentences with the correct form of the verbs in the box.**

sell spend play ~~go~~ earn buy sleep walk

1 I don't want *to go* to a bookshop.
2 We'd really like ____________ more money.
3 I wouldn't like ____________ a lot of money on a phone.
4 Yolanda would prefer not ____________ some new trainers.
5 They want ____________ video games.
6 We'd sooner ____________ less than miss the music lesson.
7 I'd rather not ____________ in the park alone at night. I think it's dangerous.

4 ★★★ **Complete the sentences with your own ideas.**

1 I'd prefer to eat ____________.
2 I wouldn't like to be ____________.
3 I don't want to go ____________.
4 I really want to be ____________.
5 In the future I would ____________.
6 I would sooner travel to ____________.

(not) enough + noun

5 ★★ **Match the sentence beginnings (1–6) with the sentence endings (a–f).**

1 We can't make a cake because *e*
2 They're not dancing here because ___
3 I can't do all my homework because ___
4 A lot of people were still hungry because ___
5 We can't all study for the exam because ___
6 We want to buy a new tablet, but ___

a there wasn't enough food.
b we haven't got enough money.
c there isn't enough space.
d I haven't got enough time.
e there aren't enough eggs.
f there aren't enough books.

6 ★★★ **Read the problems and write a sentence with (*not*) *enough*.**

1 There are five T-shirts in the shop and 20 people want to buy one.
There aren't enough T-shirts in the shop.
2 I've got £20 and these jeans cost £15.
____
3 There are a lot of children in this town and there's only one small park.
____
4 We've got 10 bottles of water for 100 people.
____
5 She's got 30 minutes before her class to do this exercise.
____
6 We're going to make sandwiches for 30 people, but we've only got 25 slices of bread.
____

Explore adjective prefixes

7 ★★ **Add the prefix *un-* to the adjectives in the box and match them with the definitions.**

friendly ~~happy~~ usual tidy fair helpful

1 sad *unhappy*
2 different or not common ____________
3 not nice to another person ____________
4 not wanting to help someone ____________
5 when the rules are not the same for everyone ____________
6 when things are not clean or not in the right place ____________

Reading

1 ★ **Read the text about a new supermarket. How is this supermarket different from others?**

SHOPPING BY PHONE

On the walls of an underground station in central Seoul, South Korea, there are a lot of pictures of food and drinks: bananas, meat, rice, coffee, even pet food. But these are not **advertisements**. This is the world's first 'virtual' supermarket, called *Homeplus*.

The supermarket is unusual because you use the special *Homeplus* app on your smartphone to go shopping. When you want to buy something, you use this **app** to scan the barcodes of the products you want. You put them in your online **shopping trolley** and then you pay by phone. You haven't got any heavy bags to carry because the supermarket **delivers** everything to your house for you.

South Koreans like shopping online and millions of them have smartphones. 'Young Koreans use their smartphones to do a lot of different **tasks** every day,' says a *Homeplus* virtual store manager. 'Our customers work really hard and don't have enough time to go to the supermarket. Our store helps them save time.' So, is this the future?

2 ★★ **Complete the definitions with the words in bold from the text.**

1 ___*Tasks*___ are little jobs we do every day at work or at home.
2 Sometimes in the middle of a TV programme, they show ___________.
3 An ___________ is a small computer program on your phone or tablet.
4 When you call a pizza company, it normally ___________ the pizzas to your house.
5 A ___________ is something you put your food in at the supermarket.

3 ★★ **Read the text again. Answer the questions.**

1 Where is the supermarket?
It's in an underground station in Seoul.
2 What can you buy at the supermarket?
____
3 What do you need to buy things here?
____
4 What happens after you pay for your shopping?
____
5 Why does the store manager think it's good for Koreans?
____

4 ★★★ **Complete the advertisement for *Homeplus* with words from the text.**

HOMEPLUS
– the virtual supermarket

We help you save time!

1 Choose the f*ood*_______ or d*rink*_______ you want.
2 Scan the b___________.
3 Fill your s___________ t___________ with food.
4 P___________ for your shopping with your p___________.
5 *Homeplus* d___________ everything to your house.

5 ★★★ **What's good about a virtual shop like this? What's bad about it? Write at least five sentences.**

____
____
____
____
____

Writing

An email

1 Read Jenny's email. What is her problem with money?

Hi Gina,
I get £5 a week pocket money, but I spend it all. How can I save my money?
Please help!
Jenny

Hi Jenny,
I have the same problem! Try writing down everything you buy for a week and how much it costs. Do you spend a lot on food and drink, for example? Don't spend money on things you don't need. Make a sandwich at home, and don't buy sweets every day.
Transfer some money into your savings account when you get it. Ask for five £1 coins so you can do this. Sometimes I try to earn some money from my family. Maybe you can do jobs, for example, wash the car or water the plants. But be realistic – £5 isn't a lot!
Good luck,
Gina

2 Complete the table with Gina's advice.

Do	Don't
write down everything you buy for a week	

Useful language Imperatives

3 Look back at Gina's email. Write the positive and negative imperatives that go before these words.

1 *Try* writing down
2 ____________ spend money
3 ____________ sweets every day
4 ____________ for five £1 coins
5 ____________ realistic

4 Put the words in order to make sentences.

1 saving / every / Try / week / something
Try saving something every week.
2 extra money / work / Do / at home / some / to earn
____
3 things / Don't / silly / money / on / spend
____
4 extra money / things / Try / to get / selling
____
5 borrow / friends / from / Don't / your / money
____

Writing

WRITING TIP

Make it better! ✓✓✓

Use *and*, *or*, *but* and *so* to make your sentences longer.

I buy sweets ***and*** *chocolate.*

I earn lots of money ***but*** *I spend it all!*

I'd like to go to Australia ***so*** *I'm saving my pocket money.*

5 Complete the sentences with *and, or, but,* or *so*.

1 Don't spend all your pocket money ___*so*___ you can save some every week.

2 Don't buy sweets, water ________ sandwiches.

3 Make your own sandwich ________ bring your own water.

4 Try selling some books ________ CDs.

5 I get £5 a week ________ I spend it all!

6 Complete the sentences with the correct preposition.

1 Don't spend a lot of money ___*on*___ sweets.

2 Ask ________ your pocket money in coins.

3 Don't borrow money ________ your friends.

4 Would you like to sell this ________ me?

5 I'm trying to save money ________ my holidays.

WRITING TIP

Make it better! ✓✓✓

If a friend has a problem, say you understand and wish them good luck.

I understand your problem. Best of luck with it.

7 Read the sentences. Which ones say you understand (*U*) and which wish someone good luck (*GL*)?

1 I hope this works for you. *GL*

2 I totally understand the problem. ____

3 That happens to me too! ____

4 Best of luck. ____

5 I wish you luck. ____

8 Read Gina's email again and tick (✓) the information she includes.

Things not to do ☑

A friendly comment to start the email ☐

A nice way to finish the email ☐

Own experience ☐

Suggestions about what to do ☐

Asking for more information ☐

A reason why something is/isn't a good idea ☐

PLAN

9 Read the question in the email below. Make notes on what information from Exercise 8 is included.

Hi everyone,
I want to earn some money for my summer holidays.
I need some ideas!
Thanks,
Freddie.

WRITE

10 Write an email to answer Freddie. Look at page 21 of the Student's Book to help you.

____

____

____

____

____

____

____

____

____

____

____

____

CHECK

11 Check your writing. Can you say YES to these questions?

- Is the information from Exercise 8 in your description?
- Do you start by saying you understand and end by wishing them luck?
- Are there positive and negative imperatives?
- Do you join sentences with *and, or, but* or *so*?
- Do you use the correct prepositions?
- Are the spelling and punctuation correct?

Do you need to write a second draft?

1 Review

Vocabulary
Shops

1 Circle the correct options.

1 A bookshop sells **books** / **sweets**.
2 A chemist sells **medicine** / **newspapers**.
3 A newsagent sells **shoes** / **comics**.
4 A sports shop sells **trainers** / **books**.
5 A music shop sells **guitars** / **computers**.
6 An electronics shop sells **laptops** / **CDs**.
7 A supermarket sells **food and drink** / **pianos**.
8 A shoe shop sells **posters** / **shoes**.
9 A department store **has got** / **hasn't got** electronics.
10 A clothes shop sells **shirts** / **cheese**.

Total: 9

Money verbs

2 Complete the text with the verbs in the box.

spend	save	earn	~~sell~~	buy	borrow

I want to [1] *sell* my old computer and [2] ___ a new one. I [3] ___ some of my money every week because I don't usually [4] ___ all of my pocket money. At the weekend, I [5] ___ money doing jobs in the garden for our neighbours. I can also [6] ___ some money from my mum and pay it back later.

Total: 5

Language focus
Present continuous

3 Complete the conversation with the present continuous form of the verbs in the box.

drink	leave	not answer	not work
buy	~~wait~~	walk	eat

Joe: Where are you? We [1] *'re waiting* for you in the café.
Tom: I [2] ___ a CD for you.
Joe: That's nice of you! Thanks! I [3] ___ hot chocolate at the moment and Sarah [4] ___ a cake.
Tom: Where's Peter? He [5] ___ his phone.
Joe: That's because his phone [6] ___ . He's here. He [7] ___ into the café right now.
Tom: Great! I [8] ___ the shop now. See you in a bit.

Total: 7

Present simple vs. continuous

4 Complete the text with the correct form of the verbs in brackets.

I usually [1] *go* (go) shopping with my friends on Saturdays. The mall [2] ___ (open) at 10:00 a.m., so we usually [3] ___ (meet) there at about 11:00. My sister [4] ___ (not go) with us. She usually [5] ___ (go) to her friend's house. She [6] ___ (stay) there until 6.00 p.m., then she [7] ___ (come) home. But today we [8] ___ (not go) anywhere. We [9] ___ (stay) at home. My sister [10] ___ (make) a cake. I [11] ___ (write) in my blog and Mum [12] ___ (listen) to music. We [13] ___ (not spend) a lot of time together at home. We sometimes [14] ___ (talk) to each other only by phone or text! So today we [15] ___ (do) something different. It [16] ___ (be) a nice change!

Total: 15

(don't) want to, would(n't) like to, would prefer to, would rather/would sooner

5 Complete the sentences with *want, like, prefer* or *'d rather*.

1 **A:** Do you *want* to go shopping?
B: I don't like shopping. I'd ___ to play volleyball.
2 **A:** Would you ___ to go cycling on Saturday?
B: No, I ___ to stay at home and play video games.
3 **A:** Do you ___ to save money?
B: Yes, but I'd also ___ to buy a new computer!
4 **A:** I think I'd ___ to sell my bicycle.
B: Great because I'd ___ to buy it!
5 **A:** I haven't got enough money. I'd ___ to borrow some from you but I'd ___ not to pay it back until next month.
B: What? No way!
6 **A:** Would you ___ to go with me to Peter's party?
B: No, I ___ not go. I don't like Peter very much.
7 **A:** I ___ be alone than have friends that don't take care about me.
B: I agree. I don't ___ to have friends that aren't actually true friends.

Total: 13

(not) enough + noun

6 Complete the sentences with *enough* and the words in the box.

people money ~~food~~ cheese homework time

1 I want to make lunch for my friends but we haven't got *enough food*.
2 My parents would like to go snowboarding this year but they haven't got ___________.
3 I need to call my grandma this morning but I haven't got ___________.
4 We'd like to start a school volleyball team but we haven't got ___________.
5 Have we got ___________ to make a pizza?
6 The teacher is angry because the students don't do their ___________.

Total: 5

Language builder

7 Circle the correct words.

Gina: I [1]___________ my new trainers today. Do you [2]___________ them?
Chris: They're great. I need [3]___________ trainers. Where [4]___________ them?
Gina: I [5]___________ them online. How about you?
Chris: I [6]___________ to the sports shop in town. I [7]___________ in town on Saturdays and there's a shop on my way home.
Gina: Have you got [8]___________ pairs of trainers?
Chris: Only two. I haven't got [9]___________ to buy more. I [10]___________ to buy another pair.
Gina: Me too!
Chris: But you [11]___________ a new pair!
Gina: Oh yeah!

1	a wear	**b** 'm wearing (circled)
2	a likes	b like
3	a some	b any
4	a do you buy	b you buy
5	a usually buy	b buy usually
6	a sometimes go	b go sometimes
7	a often am	b am often
8	a much	b many
9	a enough money	b money enough
10	a like	b 'd like
11	a wear	b 're wearing

Total: 10

Vocabulary builder

8 Complete the table with the words in the box.

~~spend~~ newsagent bowling bookshop save borrow skiing chemist cycling yoga earn supermarket department store basketball buy skateboarding karate sell

Sports	Shops	Money verbs
		spend

Total: 17

Speaking

9 Circle the correct options.

Martina: Excuse me, [1]'d like (circled) / I like to buy a T-shirt.
Shop assistant: What [2]size / number are you?
Martina: I'm a small.
Shop assistant: What about this one?
Martina: I'd [3]want / prefer a red one.
Shop assistant: A red one? Here you [4]be / are.
Martina: Can I try it on?
Shop assistant: Yes, sure. … How is it?
Martina: It's great. How [5]much / money is it?
Shop assistant: It's €6.99.
Martina: [6]I take / 'll take it.

Total: 5

Writing

10 Your friend Frank wants to save money to buy a new bike. Write a short email (30–40 words) giving him some advice on how to do that.

Total: 14

Total: 100

Get it right! Unit 1

Present simple vs. continuous

Remember that:

- we use the present simple to talk about facts, habits, routines, timetables, schedules and programmes.
- we use adverbs of frequency with the present simple.
- we use the present continuous to talk about actions in progress at the time of speaking.
- we use *at the moment* and *(right) now* with the present continuous.

1 Correct the incorrect sentences.

1. At the weekend, I'm often going shopping.
   At the weekend, I often go shopping.
2. I'm helping Mum in the kitchen right now.
   ____
3. Alex isn't here – he visits a friend at the moment.
   ____
4. I can't come to the cinema with you. I study for an important exam.
   ____
5. I've got some important news! Are you listening?
   ____
6. In my country, we are drinking a lot of tea.
   ____
7. The bank is opening at ten o'clock on Fridays.
   ____
8. Mary goes to tennis practise at ten o'clock every Saturday.
   ____

(don't) want to, would(n't) like to, would prefer to, would rather/would sooner

Remember that:

- we use the infinitive with *to* after ***want***, ***would like*** and ***would prefer***, and the infinitive without *to* after ***would rather/would sooner***.
  ✓ *I **would like to go** shopping.*
  ✗ ~~*I would like going shopping.*~~
  ✓ *He wants some tea but I'd rather have cola.*
  ✗ ~~*He wants some tea but I'd rather having cola.*~~
  ✓ *I'd sooner stay at home than go out.*
  ✗ ~~*I'd sooner staying at home than going out.*~~
- we use ***would***, not *do*, to make questions with ***would like to, would rather/would sooner*** and ***would prefer to***, but we use ***do*** to make questions with ***want***.
  ✓ ***Would you like** to come to the supermarket?*
  ✗ ~~*Do you like to come to the supermarket?*~~

2 Circle the correct words.

Jack: Hi, Emily. [1] **Do / Would** (circled: Would) you like to come shopping with me? I want [2] **buy / to buy** some new clothes for my holiday.
Emily: OK. But I [3] **don't / not** want to go to the shopping centre in town. I [4] **would / will** sooner go to the department store.
Jack: OK. We can walk to the department store, or would you [5] **want / rather** go by bike?
Emily: Well, I think I'd like [6] **going / to go** by bike.
Jack: Is 3 o'clock OK? Or [7] **will / would** you prefer to go a bit later?
Emily: Yes, 3 o'clock is fine. See you then! Bye!

Extreme adjectives

Remember that:

- we use ***very*** to make adjectives stronger.
- we don't usually use ***very*** before extreme adjectives.
  ✓ *It's **very hot** in July, but in August it's **absolutely boiling**!*
  ✗ ~~*It's absolutely hot in July, but in August it's very boiling!*~~

3 Match the sentence halves.

1. Our holiday in England was absolutely *d*
2. I'm watching the new *Batman* film. It's very ___
3. Let's go to the beach. It's absolutely ___
4. The new shopping centre is very ___

a big. c good.
b boiling! d amazing!

Spell it right! The *-ing* form

Remember that:

- for verbs ending in *-e*, we remove the *e* before we add ***-ing***: give → **giving**.
- for verbs ending with one vowel and one consonant, we **double the final** consonant: shop → **shopping**.
- for verbs ending in *-y*, we just add ***-ing***: study → **studying**.

4 Complete the sentences with the correct *-ing* form of the verb in brackets.

1. We can't play football today. It's *raining*. (rain)
2. She's ________ a letter to her penfriend. (write)
3. We go ________ every day in the holidays. I love it! (swim)
4. I don't like ________ video games. Let's go outside. (play)
5. They enjoy ________ to music on their smartphones. (listen)

2 Our heroes

General and specific competences from the curriculum explored in the unit

1. Understand oral messages in different communication situations
1.1. Identify essential information from the news presented on TV/recorded materials related to different events, when the comment is illustrated by pictures
1.2. Identify details from messages and interactions on predictable topics, when the speakers/interlocutors talk clearly and slowly
1.3. Identify specific aspects of the culture of the language studied

2. Speak in different communication situations
2.1. Present plans, intentions and future projects
2.2. Give a short and simple presentation on activities
2.3. Initiate, continue and finish a dialogue on familiar or personal interest topics
2.4. Participate in conversations related to planning activities
2.5. Show interest in participating in a verbal exchange

3. Understand written messages in different communication situations
3.1. Select necessary information from lists or simple functional texts (brochures, menus, schedules, ads)
3.2. Extract information from multiple short texts based on several predefined or negotiated criteria/constraints
3.3. Identify information from a simple written letter/email to write an answer
3.4. Show willingness to be informed through reading

4. Write messages in everyday communication situations
4.1. Complete a form with personally identifiable information (education, interests, competences)
4.2. Write a very simple personal letter (digital version included) to express thanks or apologies
4.3. Tell a story, in short, using linkers to emphasise the chronological order
4.4. Write simple and coherent texts on specific topics of interest
4.5. Participate in the exchange of written messages

Competenţele generale şi specifice din programa şcolară, urmărite în unitatea de învăţare

1. Receptarea de mesaje orale în diverse situaţii de comunicare
1.1. Identificarea informaţiilor esenţiale din ştirile prezentate la TV/materiale înregistrate, referitoare la diferite evenimente, atunci când comentariul este ilustrat prin imagini
1.2. Identificarea detaliilor din mesaje şi interacţiuni pe subiecte previzibile când locutorii/interlocutorii vorbesc clar şi rar
1.3. Identificarea unor elemente culturale specifice limbii studiate

2. Exprimarea orală în diverse situaţii de comunicare
2.1. Prezentarea unor planuri/unor intenţii şi proiecte de viitor
2.2. Descrierea scurtă, elementară a unor activităţi
2.3. Iniţierea, susţinerea şi încheierea unui dialog pe teme familiare sau de interes personal
2.4. Participarea la conversaţii în legătură cu planificarea unor activităţi
2.5. Manifestarea interesului pentru participarea la schimbul verbal

3. Receptarea de mesaje scrise în diverse situaţii de comunicare
3.1. Extragerea informaţiilor necesare din liste sau din texte funcţionale simple (pliante, meniuri, orare, reclame)
3.2. Extragerea informaţiilor din mai multe texte scurte pe baza mai multor criterii/constrângeri prestabilite sau negociate
3.3. Identificarea informaţiilor dintr-o scrisoare personală simplă/e-mail în vederea redactării unui răspuns
3.4. Manifestarea disponibilităţii pentru informare prin lectură

4. Redactarea de mesaje în diverse situaţii de comunicare
4.1. Completarea unui formular cu informaţii de identificare (educaţie, interese, competenţe)
4.2. Redactarea unei scrisori personale (inclusiv digitale) foarte simple exprimând mulţumiri sau scuze
4.3. Relatarea pe scurt a unei întâmplări utilizând cuvinte de legătură pentru a marca ordinea cronologică
4.4. Redactarea de texte simple şi coerente pe teme de interes
4.5. Participarea la schimbul de mesaje scrise

2 Our heroes

Vocabulary

Jobs

1 ★ **Find nine more jobs in the word search.**

a	s	t	m	u	n	o	t	e	r	l	w	a
c	w	r	u	b	j	u	p	i	b	d	l	s
r	e	i	s	y	o	l	k	s	e	a	n	t
p	o	l	i	c	e	o	f	f	i	c	e	r
a	l	o	c	n	g	v	f	i	l	t	m	o
d	a	f	i	t	r	v	c	r	y	o	k	n
l	i	n	a	k	u	t	h	e	s	r	t	a
w	e	s	n	u	r	s	e	f	m	o	n	u
o	d	f	b	n	u	l	s	i	e	v	e	t
c	a	h	t	r	i	w	e	g	o	p	e	r
i	n	p	o	l	r	v	e	h	a	c	r	e
s	c	i	e	n	t	i	s	t	n	o	r	s
j	e	y	o	n	e	c	h	e	r	t	h	l
q	r	z	u	i	m	x	a	r	t	i	s	t

2 ★★ **Circle the correct words in the conversation.**

A: What do you want to do when you leave school?

B: I want to be rich and famous! When I was little, I wanted to be an [1]**artist / astronaut** and travel to the moon, or a [2]**vet / nurse** and save animals' lives or work in a zoo!

A: Oh, so what are you good at?

B: Not a lot! I like acting, but I'm not very good and I can't play the guitar.

A: So you don't want to be a [3]**musician / firefighter** or [4]**an actor / a police officer**?

B: No! I don't think so. I don't think I'm very creative.

A: Well, what about a [5]**nurse / scientist** – then you can help people get better.

B: No, I think that's a difficult job. I'd really like to be [6]**an artist / a dancer** and paint beautiful pictures.

3 ★★★ **Complete the definitions with the words from Exercise 1.**

1 They move to music. You can see them in the theatre or at a concert. *dancer*
2 They find people who do bad things. ____________
3 They play the guitar, the piano or another instrument. ____________
4 You can see them in the theatre, on TV or in films. ____________
5 They work in a hospital, helping doctors. ____________
6 They paint pictures or make beautiful things. ____________
7 They help animals when they're sick. ____________
8 They travel to space and they sometimes stay there for a few months. ____________
9 They study and work in universities or laboratories. ____________
10 They help people when a building is on fire. ____________

4 ★★★ **Choose two or three jobs. What is good about them? What isn't very good? Write at least five sentences.**

It's a very interesting job. A scientist needs to study for a long time.

____

____

____

____

____

Language focus 1

was/*were*

1 ★ **Circle the correct words.**

1	I/He/She/It **was / were** there.
2	You/We/They **was / were** there.
3	I/He/She/It **wasn't / weren't** there.
4	You/We/They **wasn't / weren't** there.

2 ★★ **Complete the sentences with *was* or *were* (✓), *wasn't* or *weren't* (✗).**

1 We ___were___ (✓) both in the hockey team, but you ___________ (✓) a good player and I ___________ (✗) very good.
2 Bill Gates and Paul Allen ___________ (✗) interested in finishing their university studies. They ___________ (✓) only interested in computers.
3 Before he ___________ (✓) an actor, Hugh Jackman ___________ (✓) a PE teacher at a school.
4 Kaká ___________ (✓) always a good footballer and his brother, Digão, ___________ (✓) just like him. They ___________ (✓) both very good footballers but Kaká ___________ (✓) better.

Past simple: affirmative and negative

3 ★ **Circle the correct words.**

1	I/You/He/She/It/We/They **staying / stayed** there.
2	I/You/He/She/It/We/They **didn't stay / didn't stayed** there.
3	I/You/He/She/It/We/They **didn't go / didn't went** there.

4 ★★ **Complete the newspaper story with the past tense form of the verbs in the box.**

be not be ~~drop~~ not find go have not have look open phone pick say see take

Six months ago, 15-year-old Courtney Barwick [1]___dropped___ her wallet outside a restaurant. When she got home, she [2]___________ for it in her bag, but it [3]___________ there. Courtney went to the restaurant, but she [4]___________ the wallet. She didn't expect to see it again, but she was lucky. Someone saw it, [5]___________ it up and [6]___________ it to a bank. The wallet [7]___________ Courtney's phone number in it, so the bank [8]___________ her to tell her they had her wallet. The next day, she [9]___________ to the bank to get it. When she [10]___________ the wallet, she [11]___________ $20 inside it, and a note. The note [12]___________ 'Surprise!' and it [13]___________ a surprise, because when Courtney lost her wallet, it [14]___________ any money in it!

5 ★★★ **Your friend Paul lost something last week. Answer the questions with full sentences using the words in brackets.**

1 What did he lose? (tablet)
He lost his tablet.
2 When did he lose it? (last Friday)
____
3 What happened? (leave / on the bus)
____
4 Did he find it again? How? (Yes / the driver / pick it up)
____
5 How did he get it back? (go / bus station / get it)
____

Past simple and time expressions/adverbs

6 ★★ **Order the sentences with time expressions/adverbs. Start with the most recent.**

a I went to the shop yesterday. ___
b I did my homework this morning. _1_
c They couldn't play the piano when they were little. ___
d My parents visited Rome four days ago. ___
e They went snowboarding last month. ___

Explore expressions with *make*

7 ★★ **Match the sentence beginnings (1–6) with the sentence endings (a–f).**

1 My homework was really bad _c_
2 I like cooking so I sometimes help ___
3 When I was at the summer camp last year, ___
4 OK, you don't know what to do, ___
5 I want to do something amazing ___
6 Before you go out, ___

a I made lots of friends.
b so I can make history.
c because I made a lot of mistakes.
d so can I make a suggestion?
e make sure you do your homework.
f my mum to make a cake.

Listening and vocabulary

Adjectives of character

1 ★ **Use the clues to complete the crossword.**

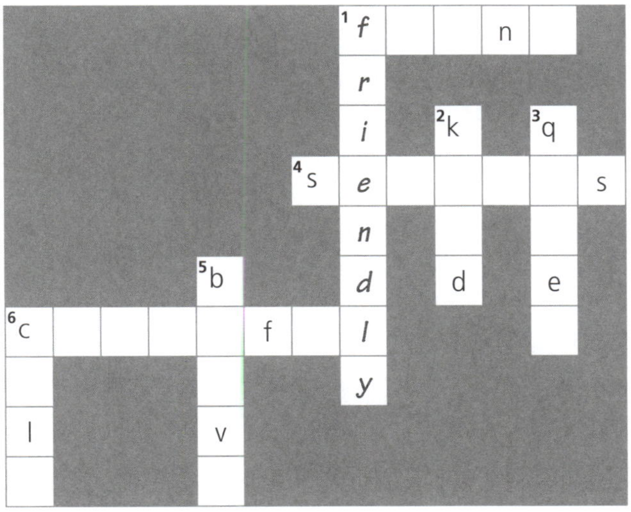

across
1 She always makes people laugh.
4 He didn't laugh or smile at all.
6 She is always happy and smiling.

down
1 The new student talked to lots of people.
2 He gave me some of his food.
3 Mark didn't say anything all evening.
5 Ellen wasn't afraid of the snake.
6 My friend never gets stressed.

2 ★★ **Circle the correct words.**

My two best friends are Chris and Adam. They are very different. Chris and I are always laughing because he is very ¹**funny** / **brave**, but Adam is very ²**cheerful** / **serious**. He doesn't smile much. A lot of people think he is unhappy but he isn't, he's quite ³**cheerful** / **kind** really! He is also a very ⁴**brave** / **quiet** person, especially at school, where he doesn't talk much. Chris is the opposite. He's ⁵**friendly** / **calm** to everyone and never stops talking! I'm not good at Science like they are, but they are both really ⁶**kind** / **serious** and help me with my homework or before an exam. Last term I was nervous before a Physics exam! Chris and Adam never panic. They told me to be ⁷**friendly** / **brave**, stay ⁸**quiet** / **calm**, and do the exam. And they were right, it wasn't a difficult exam and I passed!

Listening

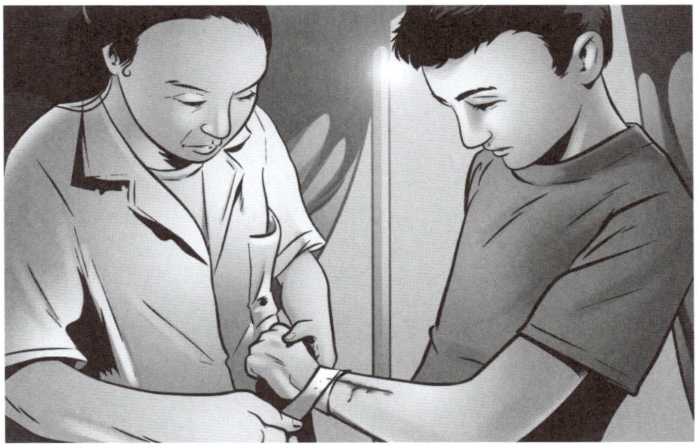

3 ★★ **Listen to the radio interview with a teenager called Jonah. What happened to him? Circle the correct option.**

a He was ill on a survival course.
b He saved his friend from the river.
c He survived a bear attack.

4 ★★ **Listen again. Circle the correct words.**

1 Two / Three teenagers were injured in a bear attack.
2 They were on a survival course in **Alaska** / **Australia**.
3 The accident happened **before** / **after** dinner.
4 When Jonah saw the bear, he **did** / **didn't do** what the instructors said.
5 The attack was very **fast** / **slow**.
6 The rescue helicopter arrived **that night** / **in the morning**.
7 Tracey Smith was **a teacher** / **a student** with the group.

5 ★★★ **Choose at least five adjectives from Exercise 1 which best describe you. Think of situations to illustrate these characteristics. Write sentences.**

I'm very funny. I made my friends laugh yesterday at breaktime.

Language focus 2

was/were: questions

1 ★ **Complete the questions and short answers in the grammar table.**

1	A:	______ you at the concert last night?
	B:	Yes, I ______.
2	A:	______ the bands good?
	B:	No, they ______.

2 ★★ **Put the words in order to make questions. Then write the answers. You can check your answers on page 20 of the Student's Book.**

1 Columbus / born / was / Where?
Where was Columbus born? In *Genoa*.

2 Anne Frank / during / was / the Second World War / Where?
______ In ______.

3 Tim Berners-Lee's / What / job / was?
______ He ______

4 family / Anne Frank / and / Who / of / were / her / afraid?
______ They ______

5 was / Columbus / 1492 / Where / in?
______ In ______

6 the / What / of / Tim Berners-Lee's / name / was / invention?
______ The ______

Past simple: questions

3 ★★ **Complete the questions to a teenager who sailed across the Atlantic alone. Use the question words and words in brackets to help you.**

How long	How many	What	~~When~~	Where

1 *When did you decide* to sail across the Atlantic? (you/ decide)
Last year.

2 ______ ? (the trip / take)
Seven weeks.

3 ______ hours ______ at night? (you / sleep)
Two or three.

4 ______ a lot of sharks? (you / see)
Yes, and dolphins.

5 ______ all day? (you / do)
I looked after the boat.

6 ______ the trip? (you / finish)
In the Caribbean.

4 ★★★ **Write questions in the past simple about the underlined information.**

1 Marie Curie won <u>the Nobel Prize for Physics</u> in 1903.
What did Marie Curie win in 1903?

2 Christopher Columbus made his fourth and final voyage <u>in 1502</u>.
______

3 Anne Frank and her family lived in those small rooms <u>for two years</u>.
______

4 Tim Berners-Lee studied <u>at Oxford</u> from 1973 to 1976.
______

5 Marie Curie was born <u>in Poland</u> in 1867.
______

6 The USA <u>made Columbus Day a holiday</u> in 1937.
______

5 ★★★ **Imagine you are interviewing Tim Berners-Lee. Read the answers and write the correct questions.**

1 *Where were you born?*
I was born in England.

2 ______
I studied Engineering at Oxford University.

3 ______
I called it the *World Wide Web* because I knew it was for the whole world.

4 ______
Oh, yes I made lots of mistakes – like the '//' in web addresses. It's really not necessary!

used to + infinitive

6 ★★ **Complete the sentences with the correct form of *used to*. Make the necessary changes.**

1 We *used to* have a dog, but now we don't.
2 Where ______ (you) go to school?
3 That bank ______ be a restaurant.
4 Sarah ______ like Paula, but now they are good friends.
5 David Beckham ______ play for Manchester United.
6 My brother ______ like History, but he does now.
7 ______ (your grandma) be a nurse?

Explore the suffix *-ness*

7 ★ **Circle the adjectives in the box that do <u>not</u> add *-ness* to make a noun.**

sad	favourite	tidy	kind	funny
~~ill~~	brilliant	happy	big	weak

Reading

The Heroes of BRITAIN

Every autumn, a TV channel organises the Pride of Britain awards ceremony. The awards ***celebrate*** people who make the world a better place and ***inspire*** others. The winners are ordinary people, but they all did something extraordinary. The programme shows a special film about each winner. They are children, teenagers and adults, people of all ages. The public, charities and the emergency services (firefighters, police, etc.) send in the names of people they want to win, and famous actors, politicians and singers present the awards.

Here are some recent winners in the ***Child of Courage*** *category:*

DANTE MARVIN – 2019 (11 at that time)

Dante has brittle bone disease and scoliosis and needs a ***wheelchair***, but he refuses to let it get him down. He tells everyone he meets: 'There are no ***disabilities***, only abilities.' He started working closely with children's charity *Variety* after his mum asked for help to buy a new wheelchair. The charity was so impressed with Dante's positive attitude, it invited him to become a Young Ambassador.

FREYA HARRIS – 2023 (8 at that time)

Freya formed a heartwarming ***bond*** with her dog Echo after being diagnosed with Stage 4 cancer in 2021. Her parents got her an Australian Shepherd puppy to encourage her to go for walks after spending time in hospital for treatment. Despite ***challenges*** with her health, she didn't give up and participated in Crufts, the world's greatest dog show, becoming an inspiration for millions of people.

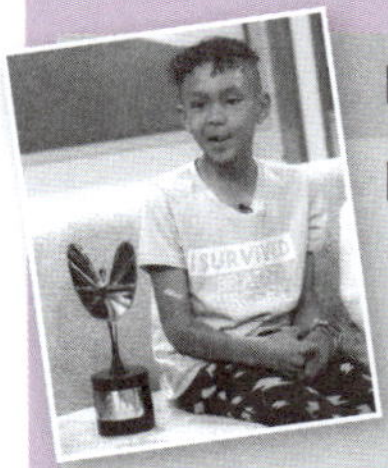

RAVI ADELEKAN – 2023 (8 at that time)

Ravi is a schoolboy with a million dreams. But, at the age of 6, his dreams were interrupted by a surgery to remove a non-cancerous tumour from his brain stem. Doctors were not able to remove the whole tumour, so Ravi had to learn to walk and feed himself again. With the support from friends and the local community, he started to help others with a similar condition. Ravi's dream is to have a future where tumours like his could be treated without the type of major surgery he went through.

1 ★ **Read the text about a special TV programme. Tick (✓) the kind of people in the programme.**

actors and singers	☐	sportspeople	☐
children	✓	brave people	☐
teenagers	☐	heroes	☐

2 ★ **Look at the words in bold in the text. What kind of words (noun or verb) are they?**

1 celebrate *verb*
2 inspire ____
3 wheelchair ____
4 disability ____
5 bond ____
6 challenges ____

3 ★★ **Complete the definitions with the correct form of the words from Exercise 2.**

1 A person who can't walk needs a *wheelchair*.
2 A ____ is something new and difficult which requires great effort and determination.
3 A ____ is an illness or injury that makes it difficult to do things other people can do.
4 Sometimes you want to do something because someone ____ you to do it.
5 When we say we admire someone and show them how much we like them, we ____ them.
6 A ____ is a close connection between two or more people or things.

4 ★★ **Read the text again. Circle the correct answer for each question.**

1 When can you see the *Pride of Britain* awards ceremony?
   (a) once a year b every four years c in the summer
2 What type of people win these awards?
   a famous actors b people who helped others c politicians
3 Who doesn't send in names of people to win the awards?
   a the public b singers c police or ambulance workers
4 Who uses a wheelchair?
   a Dante b Freya c Ravi
5 Who has a dog as a close companion?
   a Dante b Freya c Ravi
6 Who wants tumours to be treated in a different way in the future?
   a Dante b Freya c Ravi

5 ★★★ **Is there an award like the *Pride of Britain* in your country? Do you know about anyone who is an 'ordinary' hero? What did they do?**

Writing

A description of a person you admire

1 Read Patrick's description of a person he admires. Why was Judith by the river?

One person I admire is Judith, a girl who lives on my street. She's older than I am, but she's in my sister's class and they're in the same swimming club as well.

She's got a dog so she often takes it for walks by the river at the back of our house. Last winter a small boy fell into the river and couldn't swim. Judith heard him scream and didn't stop to think. Although the water was very cold, she jumped in to rescue him. The boy disappeared under the water, but Judith stayed calm and pulled him out. A neighbour saw them and went to help them get out of the water. They were both fine after they got warm again.

I admire her because she saved the boy's life, but she says it was nothing special! She is very brave. The boy's parents think she is a hero and I agree.

2 Read the description again. Answer the questions.

1 How does Patrick know Judith? ____________
2 Why did the boy scream? ____________
3 What did Judith do? ____________
4 What happened when they were in the water? ____________
5 What does Judith think about what happened? ____________

Useful language Connectors

3 Look back at the text. Which words does Patrick use to join these ideas? Where do they go in the sentence?

1 My sister and Judith are in the same class. They are in the same swimming club.
and (in the middle), as well (at the end)
2 She's got a dog. She often takes it for walks by the river.
____
3 The water was very cold. She jumped in to rescue him.
____
4 I admire her. She saved the boy's life.
____

4 Join the sentences using the connectors in brackets.

1 The bag was very heavy. He carried it for her. (although)
Although the bag was very heavy, he carried it for her.
2 We live in the same street. We go to the same school. (and, as well)
____
3 We both like music. We decided to start a band together. (so)
____
4 The man couldn't get up the stairs. He was in a wheelchair. (because)
____

5 Look back at the text. Find apostrophes and match them with their uses.

1 *She's* = She is
2 ____________ = possession
3 ____________ = they are
4 ____________ = could not
5 ____________ = She has

6 Write apostrophes in the correct place in the sentences.

1 They're my sister's best friends.
2 Shes a real hero because she saved the boys life.
3 Were in the same class so were the same age.
4 Life wasnt easy for her because she didnt use to have a lot of money.
5 Id like to be like him when Im older.

Writing

WRITING TIP

Make it better! ✓✓✓
Use the infinitive with *to* to explain the purpose of an action (why someone did something).
I went to the shop to buy some bread.

7 Complete the sentences with the infinitive form of the verbs in the box.

make	work	become	rescue
~~help~~	find out	earn	

1 She heard a girl shout so she ran *to help* her.
2 We called our friend ___________ what happened.
3 He studied very hard ___________ a doctor.
4 They worked very hard ___________ enough money.
5 He climbed the tree ___________ the cat.
6 Gary went slowly ___________ sure he didn't fall.
7 He used ___________ as a firefighter. He saved many lives.

WRITING TIP

Make it better! ✓✓✓
Write about the person's character – use adjectives to say what the person is like.
My aunt can be quite serious, but she's very kind, too.

8 Read the sentences. Which one does <u>not</u> describe someone's character?

1 She's really friendly and she talks to everyone.
2 Linda is kind and always finds time for her friends.
3 My uncle is very brave, but he doesn't think so.
4 He's quite young and he's tall and strong.
5 Robbie always tells jokes – he's really funny.

9 Look back at Patrick's description. Order the things he talks about.

what other people think of him/her
~~who the person is~~ why you admire them
how you know the person what the person did
the person's character

1 *who the person is*
2 ___________
3 ___________
4 ___________
5 ___________
6 ___________

PLAN

10 Choose a person you know and admire to write about. Use the things in Exercise 9 and make notes.

WRITE

11 Write the description of the person you chose in Exercise 10. Look at page 31 of the Student's Book to help you.

____
____
____
____
____
____
____
____
____
____
____
____

CHECK

12 Check your writing. Can you say YES to these questions?

- Is the information from Exercise 9 in your description?
- Do you describe the person's character and say why you admire them?
- Do you use connectors to join sentences?
- Do you use the infinitive with *to* to explain the purpose?
- Do you use apostrophes correctly?
- Are the spelling and punctuation correct?

Do you need to write a second draft?

2 Review

Vocabulary
Jobs

1 Match the words in the box with the jobs in the pictures.

dancer police officer musician actor nurse artist vet ~~astronaut~~ scientist firefighter

1 astronaut

2 __________

3 __________

4 __________

5 __________

6 __________

7 __________

8 __________

9 __________

10 __________

Total: 9

Adjectives of character

2 Circle the correct words.

1 I don't like going to the dentist. I'm not very **brave** / **friendly**.
2 Ellen usually laughs and smiles all day. She's very **funny** / **cheerful**.
3 Steven doesn't like talking. He's very **calm** / **quiet**.
4 Jessie always helps me with my homework. He's very **kind** / **stubborn**.
5 Jenny isn't nervous about exams. She's very **calm** / **serious**.
6 Max works hard at school. He's very **serious** / **brave**.
7 His stories always make me laugh. He's very **cheerful** / **funny**.

Total: 6

Language focus
was/were and past simple: affirmative and negative

3 Complete the sentences with the past form of the verbs in brackets.

1 I __was__ born in Switzerland and I __________ to school in France. (be, go)
2 Bill __________ Science, but he __________ good at languages. (study, not be)
3 Jane __________ around the world and __________ a book about her journey. (sail, write)
4 Maria __________ music, but she __________ a famous singer. (not study, become)
5 Danny __________ good at art, but he __________ to be an artist. (be, not want)

Total: 9

Past simple: questions

4 Write a question for each answer.

1 **A:** Where / born?
Where were you born? ____________________
B: I was born in Italy.

2 **A:** What / study?
B: She studied Geography.

3 **A:** They / good at sport?
B: No, they weren't good at sport.

4 **A:** You / play tennis at school?
B: Yes, we did.

Total: 3

used to + infinitive

5 Write questions with *used to* and the words in brackets.

1 **A:** *Where did you use to spend your holidays?* (spend, holidays)
B: At the seaside.

2 **A:** ____________________ (be, best friend)?
B: Ben Spencer.

3 **A:** ____________________? (play, as a child)
B: On the street, with my friends.

4 **A:** ____________________? (hobbies, have)
B: I used to play cricket ten years ago.

Total: 3

Language builder

6 Choose the correct options.

Cheryl: What [1]__________ yesterday? [2]__________ you busy?
Jake: I [3]__________ in the music shop on Saturday mornings. It [4]__________ really busy on Saturdays.
Cheryl: Do you like [5]__________ there?
Jake: Yes, I [6]__________. But yesterday I [7]__________ up late and then I [8]__________ late for work.
Cheryl: Oh no!
Jake: The manager [9]__________ very happy!
Cheryl: Do you play [10]__________ musical instruments?
Jake: Yes, I [11]__________ to play the guitar.

1	a	are you doing	(b)	did you do
2	a	Was	b	Were
3	a	work	b	works
4	a	is usually	b	usually is
5	a	work	b	working
6	a	am	b	do
7	a	got	b	get
8	a	am	b	was
9	a	wasn't	b	weren't
10	a	any	b	much
11	a	learn	b	'm learning

Total: 10

Vocabulary builder

7 Choose the correct options.

1 You can sometimes __________ extra pocket money by washing cars.
(a) earn b spend c borrow

2 A __________ studies Chemistry, Physics, or Biology.
a scientist b dancer c writer

3 You can usually buy magazines in __________.
a a shoe shop b a newsagent
c a clothes shop

4 Bill isn't scared. He's very __________.
a serious b cheerful c brave

5 I'm trying to __________ money by not buying chocolate.
a spend b save c earn

6 __________ creates pictures and paintings.
a An actor b An artist
c An astronaut

7 Nina helps other people. She is very __________.
a serious b quiet c kind

8 You can buy medicine in __________.
a an electronics shop b a sports shop
c a chemist

Total: 7

Speaking

8 Complete the conversation with the words in the box.

look	may	That	~~think~~	maybe	sure

Luke: Who do you [1]*think* it is?
Oli: I'm not [2]__________. He [3]__________ be a footballer.
Luke: No, he doesn't [4]__________ very sporty.
Oli: OK, then [5]__________ he's a singer.
Luke: [6]__________ 's possible.

Total: 5

Total: 47

Get it right! Unit 2

was/were

1 Complete the text with *was* or *were*.

Yesterday, my mum [1] _*was*_ at the shopping mall all afternoon. My dad and my brother [2] ______ at a football match. So I [3] ______ at home alone. I watched a couple of programmes on TV, but they [4] ______ boring. I texted my friends, Anna and Maria, but they [5] ______ both busy. I started my homework, but it [6] ______ too difficult.

Spell it right! Shopping words

Remember to spell these clothes and shopping words correctly.

shopping	~~shoping~~	trainers	~~trainners~~
bought	~~bougth~~	trousers	~~trausers~~
expensive	~~spensive~~	T-shirt	~~T-shir~~

was/were: questions

Remember that:

- we make questions with ***was/were*** before the subject.
  ✓ ***Were you*** *at home last night?*
  ✗ ~~*You were at home last night?*~~
- we make information questions with the *Wh-* question word + ***was/were*** + subject.
  ✓ ***Where were you*** *last night?*
  ✗ ~~*Where you were last night?*~~
- we make questions with *how many* + subject + ***was/were***.
  ✓ ***How many students were*** *in your class?*
  ✗ ~~*How many were students in your class?*~~

2 Read the sentences about a party. Write the correct questions. Use *was/were*.

1 I was at a party on Saturday night.
Where were you on Saturday night ______?

2 The party was at Mary's house.
______?

3 No, I wasn't late. I arrived at 8 o'clock.
______?

4 There were 20 people at the party.
______?

5 Yes, Peter and his brother were at the party.
______?

6 I was at the party for three hours.
______?

7 Yes, all the people at the party were happy.
______?

Jobs

Remember that:

- we use ***a*** or ***an*** to talk about a person who does a particular job.
  ✓ *My brother wants to be* ***a*** *firefighter.*
  ✗ ~~*My brother wants to be firefighter.*~~
- we use ***a*** before consonants and ***an*** before vowel sounds.

3 Read the text. Add *a* or *an* in the correct places.

My friend James has got two brothers. Their dad is ^*a* famous artist and their mum is vet. But the brothers don't want to be artists or vets. James wants to be actor because he loves the theatre. His brother, Paul, would like to be firefighter or astronaut, but he isn't tall enough, so he wants to be police officer. And his younger brother, Michael, loves music, but he can't be singer, because he can't sing. But he plays the piano very well, so, maybe he will be musician.

Expressions with *make*

Remember, some nouns have ***make*** before them, but other nouns have ***do*** before them.

✓ *I want to* ***make a cake*** *for my sister's birthday.*
✗ ~~*I want to do a cake for my sister's birthday.*~~
✓ *Police officers make sure people don't* ***do bad things****.*
✗ ~~*Police officers make sure people don't make bad things.*~~

4 Complete the sentences with *make* or *do*.

1 Arturo didn't ___*do*___ his homework yesterday.
2 I'd like to ______ a suggestion.
3 What job do you want to ______ when you leave school?
4 What sports do you ______ in your free time?
5 I want to ______ friends with new people from different countries.
6 They like speaking English, but they often ______ mistakes.
7 Sara is ill, so she can't ______ the exam.
8 She works hard and helps people because she wants to ______ a difference.

3 At home

General and specific competences from the curriculum explored in the unit

1. Understand oral messages in different communication situations
1.1. Identify essential information from the news presented on TV/recorded materials related to different events, when the comment is illustrated by pictures
1.2. Identify details from messages and interactions on predictable topics, when the speakers/interlocutors talk clearly and slowly
1.3. Identify specific aspects of the culture of the language studied

2. Speak in different communication situations
2.1. Present plans, intentions and future projects
2.2. Give a short and simple presentation on activities
2.3. Initiate, continue and finish a dialogue on familiar or personal interest topics
2.4. Participate in conversations related to planning activities
2.5. Show interest in participating in a verbal exchange

3. Understand written messages in different communication situations
3.1. Select necessary information from lists or simple functional texts (brochures, menus, schedules, ads)
3.2. Extract information from multiple short texts based on several predefined or negotiated criteria/constraints
3.3. Identify information from a simple written letter/email to write an answer
3.4. Show willingness to be informed through reading

4. Write messages in everyday communication situations
4.1. Complete a form with personally identifiable information (education, interests, competences)
4.2. Write a very simple personal letter (digital version included) to express thanks or apologies
4.3. Tell a story, in short, using linkers to emphasise the chronological order
4.4. Write simple and coherent texts on specific topics of interest
4.5. Participate in the exchange of written messages

Competenţele generale și specifice din programa școlară, urmărite în unitatea de învățare

1. Receptarea de mesaje orale în diverse situaţii de comunicare
1.1. Identificarea informaţiilor esențiale din știrile prezentate la TV/materiale înregistrate, referitoare la diferite evenimente, atunci când comentariul este ilustrat prin imagini
1.2. Identificarea detaliilor din mesaje și interacţiuni pe subiecte previzibile când locutorii/interlocutorii vorbesc clar și rar
1.3. Identificarea unor elemente culturale specifice limbii studiate

2. Exprimarea orală în diverse situaţii de comunicare
2.1. Prezentarea unor planuri/unor intenţii și proiecte de viitor
2.2. Descrierea scurtă, elementară a unor activități
2.3. Inițierea, susținerea și încheierea unui dialog pe teme familiare sau de interes personal
2.4. Participarea la conversaţii în legătură cu planificarea unor activităţi
2.5. Manifestarea interesului pentru participarea la schimbul verbal

3. Receptarea de mesaje scrise în diverse situaţii de comunicare
3.1. Extragerea informaţiilor necesare din liste sau din texte funcţionale simple (pliante, meniuri, orare, reclame)
3.2. Extragerea informațiilor din mai multe texte scurte pe baza mai multor criterii/constrângeri prestabilite sau negociate
3.3. Identificarea informaţiilor dintr-o scrisoare personală simplă/e-mail în vederea redactării unui răspuns
3.4. Manifestarea disponibilităţii pentru informare prin lectură

4. Redactarea de mesaje în diverse situaţii de comunicare
4.1. Completarea unui formular cu informaţii de identificare (educaţie, interese, competenţe)
4.2. Redactarea unei scrisori personale (inclusiv digitale) foarte simple exprimând mulțumiri sau scuze
4.3. Relatarea pe scurt a unei întâmplări utilizând cuvinte de legătură pentru a marca ordinea cronologică
4.4. Redactarea de texte simple și coerente pe teme de interes
4.5. Participarea la schimbul de mesaje scrise

3 At home

Vocabulary

Things in the home

1 ★ **Look at the pictures of the things in the home. Write the words in the correct column. Some words can go in more than one column.**

living room	bedroom	bathroom	other rooms
	mirror	*mirror*	

2 ★★ **Complete the sentences with the words from Exercise 1.**

1 Where's my dictionary? It isn't on my *desk* or on the ______ with the other books.
2 My dad has two ______ on his bed because he says it's comfortable, but I only have one.
3 In winter, I always sleep with a big ______ to keep warm.
4 Houses in the UK usually have ______ on the floor.
5 My little sister can't see herself in our bathroom ______ because she's too short.
6 My mum and dad have got a lot of clothes so their ______ is full.
7 Can you get the sugar? It's in the ______, in the kitchen.
8 When I wake up in the morning, I open the ______ and look outside.

3 ★★★ **Mark and Jane are in their new house, but it's empty. Read the sentences and write what they need to buy.**

1 'We haven't got anywhere to put our clothes!' *wardrobe*
2 'There's nothing on the floor and it's very cold.' ______
3 'We've got plates and glasses for the kitchen but nowhere to put them.' ______
4 'I just washed my hands, but I can't dry them.' ______
5 'Our neighbours can see us through the windows!' ______
6 'We've got nothing on the bed.' ______, ______
7 'I need a place to work and somewhere to put my books.' ______, ______
8 'I can't believe we can't wash the plates and glasses!' ______

4 ★★★ **What's your favourite room in your home? Why do you like it? What furniture does it have? What other furniture would you like to have? Write at least five sentences.**

My favourite room is my bedroom. I like it because it's a big, sunny room.

Language focus 1

Comparatives and superlatives

1 ★ Complete the rules in the grammar table.

-ier   worse   more (x2)   Better   ~~two~~   *-er*

1	We use comparative adjectives to compare *two* or more people, things, etc.
2	To form the comparative of short adjectives (one syllable), we add ____________.
3	To form the comparative of long adjectives (two syllables +), we use ____________ before the adjective.
4	When the adjective has two syllables and ends in *-y*, we remove the *-y* and add ____________ to form the comparative.
5	____________ (good) and ____________ (bad) are irregular comparatives.
6	To make the comparative form of an adverb we usually add ____________.

2 ★★ Write comparative sentences.

1 The Empire State Building / high / the Eiffel Tower
The Empire State Building is higher than the Eiffel Tower.
2 Buckingham Palace / big / the White House
3 His desk / expensive / all our furniture
4 A bed / comfortable / a sofa
5 The hotel in Santiago / good / the hotel in Buenos Aires
6 Gail's room / tidy / Kerry's

3 ★ Choose the correct options to complete the grammar table.

1	To form the superlative of short adjectives (one syllable), we add *-er* / *-est* (circled)
2	To form the superlative of long adjectives (two syllables +), we use *more* / *most* before the adjective.
3	When the adjective has two syllables and ends in *-y*, we remove the *-y* and add *-est* / *-iest* to form the superlative.
4	*Best* / *The best* and *worst* / *the worst* are irregular superlatives.

4 ★ Complete the text with the superlative form of the adjectives in the box.

big   expensive   ~~rich~~   tall   ugly   unusual

The billionaire Mukesh Ambani is [1] *the richest* man in India. He and his family live in a house called Antilia, in Mumbai, India. Antilia cost one billion dollars! It's [2] ____________ house in the world – a tower with 27 floors. It's also [3] ____________ family home in the world. There are three floors of gardens and it has [4] ____________ garage in a family house too, with space for 168 cars, all for Mr Ambani's family of six! Antilia is modern, but it isn't beautiful. In fact, many people think it's [5] ____________ building in Mumbai. I'm not sure about that, but it's probably [6] ____________ billionaire's house in the world!

5 ★★★ Write the sentences in the comparative or superlative.

1 Mount Everest / high / mountain / in the world
Mount Everest is the highest mountain in the world.
2 This pillow / soft / that pillow
3 The library / quiet / place in the school
4 The beach / relaxing / place to go in the summer
5 A holiday in New York / good / a holiday at home
6 My dad's car / small / my mum's car

Explore expressions with *do*

6 ★★ Match the sentence beginnings (1–6) with the sentence endings (a–f).

1 Could you do me a favour? *c*
2 Can I help you with your homework? ___
3 My dad can't play football with me ___
4 I didn't go out on Saturday because ___
5 Paul was really tired last night because ___
6 We put all the food in the cupboard ___

a I had a lot of homework to do.
b after we did the shopping.
c Could you give me that book on the shelf?
d because he's doing the housework.
e he did sport for three hours.
f I like doing Maths.

Listening and vocabulary

UNIT 3

Household appliances

1 ★ **Add vowels to make words for household appliances. Write them under the correct picture.**

dshwshr	frzr	rn	~~frdg~~	wshng mchn
lmp	hrdryr	ckr	htr	

1 *fridge*

2 ____________

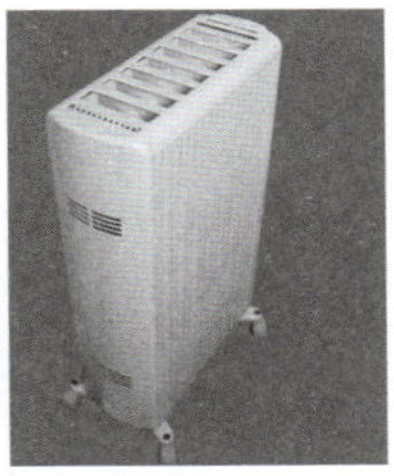

3 ____________

4 ____________

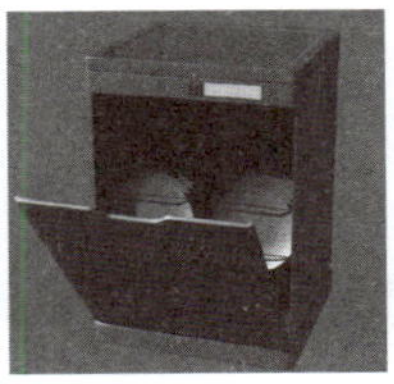

5 ____________

6 ____________

7 ____________

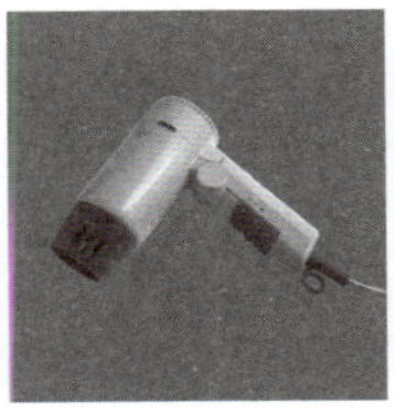

8 ____________

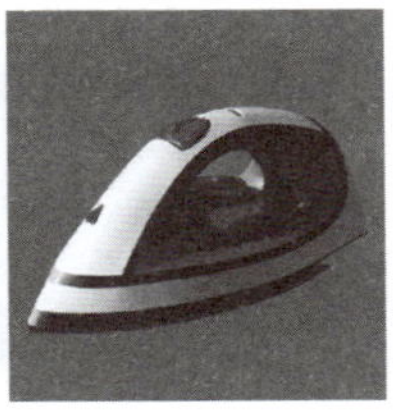

9 ____________

2 ★★ **Match the words from Exercise 1 with the sentences.**

1 You use this when your hair is wet. *hairdryer*
2 This washes your clothes. ____________
3 It keeps food cool and safe to eat. ____________
4 It helps you see in the dark. ____________
5 You use this when your house is cold. ____________
6 It cleans the plates and glasses. ____________
7 It makes your clothes look nice. ____________
8 You use this to cook your dinner. ____________
9 You can leave food in it for a long time. ____________

3 ★★★ **Complete the text with the words from Exercise 1.**

The room with the most appliances in our house is the kitchen. I use the 1 *cooker* every evening to make dinner.

We also use the 2 ____________ once a day to wash our clothes, and the 3 ____________ every day to clean the plates.

Of course, we always use the 4 ____________ to keep our food cool and fresh. When my mum cooks, she often puts the extra food in the 5 ____________. She says it can stay there for months. One thing I never use is the 6 ____________. My mum hates this too, so my dad uses it for his shirts and my T-shirts.

Another thing I use every day is the 7 ____________ on my desk – it helps me to see my books because my room is quite dark. And when it's cold, I sometimes use the 8 ____________ to stay warm! I've got long hair so I also use my 9 ____________ every day.

Listening

4 ★ **Listen to the conversation between Ella and Nick. What are they talking about?**

5 ★★ **Listen again. Mark the sentences true (*T*) or false (*F*).**

1 Ella and Nick are brother and sister. *T*
2 They went to see three flats. ___
3 One flat is really old. ___
4 Both flats had two bathrooms. ___
5 Ella likes the first flat better. ___
6 Nick and Ella usually catch the bus to school. ___
7 Their mum and dad want to plan a new bedroom. ___
8 Nick isn't sure the flat is big enough. ___

Language focus 2

should/shouldn't for giving advice and making suggestions

1 ★ **Circle the correct words.**

1	We use *should* and *shouldn't* + verb / *to* + verb.
2	We use ***should / shouldn't*** to talk about what is the ideal or best thing to do in a situation.
3	We use ***should / shouldn't*** to make suggestions not to do something.
4	We use ***should and shouldn't*** to give advice / talk about obligation and prohibition.

2 ★★ **Complete the text with *should* or *shouldn't*.**

Feng shui is the old Chinese art of organising your home to bring good health and energy. Here are some ideas about how to improve your house:

- In the bedroom you [1] *should* always clean under the bed so you don't have negative energy. You [2] ______ keep anything there. The bed [3] ______ never be close to the door or under a window.
- In the living room you [4] ______ put a mirror on the wall to give your house more energy, and you [5] ______ have a plant to show love.
- The colour red is good luck, but you [6] ______ have too much of it because it can make people nervous. Finally, you [7] ______ leave space around the things in the house so energy can move around the room.

Do these things and you [8] ______ have any problems!

3 ★★★ **Complete the second sentence so it has the same meaning as the first. Use *should* or *shouldn't*.**

1 It's a good idea for them to try feng shui.
They *should try feng shui.*

2 It's not a very good idea to do her homework in the kitchen.
She ______

3 The best thing we can do is to leave it until tomorrow; it's late now.
We ______.

4 My advice is to put your desk under the window.
I think you ______.

5 I suggest him not to speak to his parents in that way.
He ______.

4 ★★★ **Complete the sentences about your life at home.**

1 My parents say I should *be quicker in the bathroom in the morning, because I'm sometimes late for school.*

2 My ______ says I should't ______

3 I should ______

4 I shouldn't ______

5 ★ **Complete the rules in the grammar table**

1 We use ______ to ask permission to do something.	
2 We use ______ to ask someone else to do something.	
3 To ask questions, we put *can* and *will* ______ the subject.	

can, will for making a polite request

6 ★★ **Complete the sentences with *can* or *will* and a verb from the box.**

sit ~~go~~ use tell open

1 I finished my homework. *Can* I *go* now?

2 ______ you ______ Sally I called her?

3 ______ I ______ your computer?

4 Hello. ______ you ______ the door for me, please?

5 ______ I ______ here?

Explore verbs with *up* or *down*

7 ★★ **Complete the sentences with the correct form of the verbs in the box and *up* or *down*.**

go lie come (x2) put

1 Why did you climb that wall? You should *come down* now.

2 Oh no, it's raining. Can you ______ the umbrella?

3 We woke up early and watched the sun ______.

4 You look tired. Why don't you go and ______ on your bed?

5 The shops are near here. ______ to the top of the road and turn left.

Reading

1 ★ **Read the texts and match the people with the houses in the pictures.**

1 ____________

2 ____________

3 ____________

2 ★★ **Match the words in bold in the text with the definitions.**

1 It's a game where some people hide while one person counts to 100. That person then tries to find everyone. *hide and seek*
2 The same shape as a ball or a circle. ____________
3 The parts of a room above your head. ____________
4 A windmill usually has four of these and they move in the wind. ____________
5 To make something full or put things in an empty space. ____________
6 Chairs, tables, bed, etc. ____________

Unusual place to live

Joey
I live in a windmill! It has five floors and a lot of stairs. The kitchen is at the bottom, the living room is on the first floor, and my bedroom is at the top. It's noisy because of the ***sails*** in the wind, especially in the winter, but the strangest thing is that the rooms are ***round***. Mine is the smallest. It's really difficult to find space for all my things. It's fun here though, and the view is amazing!

Abigail
My friends are always surprised that I live in a 300-year-old house! When my parents bought our house, it was a mess, but now it's beautiful. There are 80 large rooms and 40 bedrooms, so we need a lot of ***furniture*** to ***fill*** it. It's a great place for parties, and playing ***hide and seek***, but it's easy to get lost!

David
My home is a traditional cottage in a country village. I live here with my parents and my two sisters. It's prettier than my friends' houses, but it's very old, so all the rooms are small and uncomfortable, and the ***ceilings*** are low. Also, there's only one bathroom, but my parents love it! My room is in the attic. It's very small, and the floor is not very straight. There's only a bed, a cupboard and a small desk under the window.

3 ★★ **Read the text again. Which house is each sentence about? Write *Joey*, *Abigail* or *David*.**

1 The house has a lot of different floors. *Joey*
2 It's good for games. ____________
3 It's a strange shape. ____________
4 Visitors can choose a room to sleep in. ____________
5 It's not good for a big family. ____________
6 It isn't quiet. ____________
7 Tall people can't live in a house like this. ____________
8 It wasn't always a nice house. ____________

4 ★★★ **Which of these houses would you like to live in? Why? Do you think your family would like it too? Why/Why not? Write at least five sentences.**

____
____
____
____
____

Writing

A description of a house

1 Read Corrine's email about an unusual house. Why is she there?

YourMAIL | (+) New | Reply | ▾ | Delete | Junk | ▾

Hi Emma,

How are you? We're staying in a really unusual holiday home for two weeks. It's a tall, old, white lighthouse in Somerset. It's 33 metres high with 120 stairs! There are eight floors with three bedrooms, a living room, a big, modern kitchen and a bathroom. The bedrooms all have small, new showers and the views of the sea are amazing. All the walls are round of course, but the rooms are bigger than you think. The top floor has the big, old light, but it doesn't work now. The lighthouse is 180 years old, but everything is modern inside and there's even wi-fi. What do you think? Isn't it amazing?!

Love, Corrine

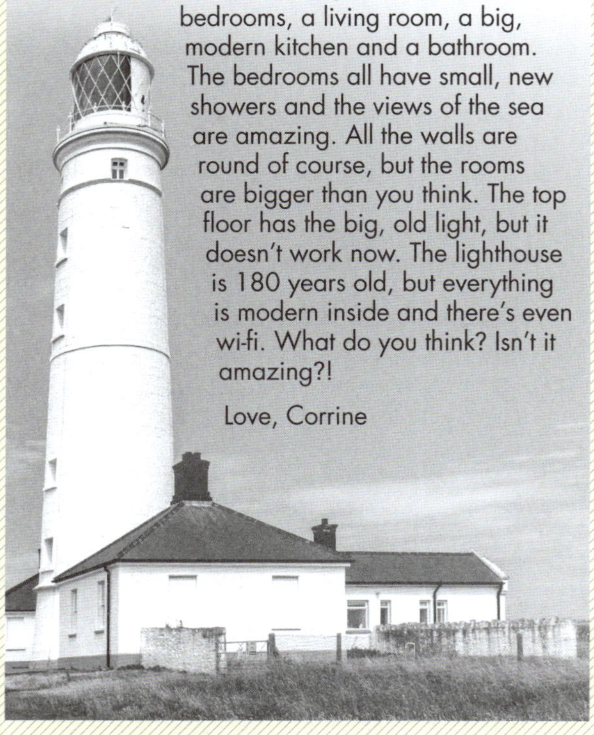

2 Read the email again. What do these numbers mean?

1 120 = *stairs in the lighthouse*
2 8 = ____________
3 2 = ____________
4 180 = ____________
5 33 = ____________

Useful language Order of adjectives

3 Read the email again. Write the adjectives.

1 a *tall*, ________, ________ lighthouse
2 a ________, ________ kitchen
3 ________, ________ showers
4 the ________, ________ light

4 Put the words in order to make sentences.

1 old / There's / tall / wardrobe / a / white
There's a tall, old, white wardrobe.
2 has got / living room / lamp / small / a / The / yellow / modern
____
3 has got / a / bed / My / old / bedroom / large
____
4 red and blue / The / got / four / big / pillows / bed's / new
____
5 on his desk / a / photo / tiny / black and white / old / There's
____

WRITING TIP

Make it better! ✓ ✓ ✓
Use comparatives and superlatives to describe the things in your house.
My sister's bedroom is bigger than mine.

5 Complete the sentences with the comparative or superlative form of the adjectives in brackets.

1 The bathrooms are *smaller than* the bedrooms. (small)
2 My parents have got ________ bedroom in the house. (large)
3 The wardrobe is ________ my bathroom! (big)
4 The furniture in her house is ________ the furniture in my house. (modern)
5 The apartment has got ________ views of the city. (beautiful)

6 Complete the sentences with two or three adjectives to describe the rooms in your house.

1 We've got a *small, new* kitchen.
2 There's a ________ bedroom.
3 There's a ________ living room.
4 I've got a ________ bathroom.

Writing

WRITING TIP

Make it better! ✓✓✓

Give your opinion of the place, the house or the rooms.

It's a small house, but I really like it because it's warm and comfortable.

7 Which of these sentences does not give an opinion?

1 The house is really unusual.
2 The gardens are really beautiful.
3 There are three large bedrooms.
4 It's really relaxing to walk on the beach near the house.

8 Read Corrine's email again and tick (✓) the information she includes.

a what rooms there are ☐
b the number of bedrooms ☐
c what her favourite room is and why ☐
d what she does in each room ☐
e how old/big the house is ☐
f interesting or unusual features/furniture ☐

PLAN

9 Choose one of these holiday homes to write an email about. Use the information in Exercise 8 and make notes in your notebook.

a castle in England

a stone cottage in Ireland

a luxury flat in a big city

a houseboat in the Netherlands

WRITE

10 Write the email. Look at page 45 of the Student's Book to help you.

____
____
____
____
____
____
____
____
____
____
____
____

CHECK

11 Check your writing. Can you say YES to these questions?

- Is the information from Exercise 8 in your description?
- Do you use adjectives to describe the room and things in the place?
- Do you use comparative and superlative sentences?
- Do you give your opinion of the place, the rooms or the things?

Do you need to write a second draft?

3 Review

Vocabulary

Things in the home

1 Match the words in the box to the definitions.

sink towel mirror blanket curtains pillow wardrobe ~~carpet~~ shelf cupboard desk

1. This is on the floor. You walk on it. *carpet*
2. You open these in the morning so you can see outside. ______
3. This is on the bed. It's for your head. ______
4. This is in the bathroom. You use it after a shower. ______
5. This is in the bathroom. You can see yourself in it. ______
6. You put all your clothes in here. ______
7. You put plates, cups, glasses, or food in here. ______
8. This is on the bed. You use it when it's cold. ______
9. You put books on this. ______
10. This is in your bedroom. You do your homework here. ______
11. This is in the kitchen. You wash dirty plates in here. ______

Total: 10

Household appliances

2 Complete the sentences with words in the box.

dishwasher ~~washing machine~~ fridge heater lamp cooker hairdryer freezer iron

1. Put the dirty clothes into the *washing machine*.
2. It's cold! Turn on the ______.
3. Take some ice out of the ______.
4. Put the milk back in the ______.
5. I'd like to cook dinner. Turn on the ______.
6. Your hair is wet. Go and get the ______.
7. Put the dirty plates into the ______.
8. Oh no! I burned my shirt with the ______!
9. I can't see. It's very dark. Turn on the ______.

Total: 8

Language focus

Comparatives

3 Write comparative sentences.

1. London / Edinburgh (big)
   London is bigger than Edinburgh.
2. Cheetahs / elephants (fast)
   ______
3. The Amazon / the Danube (long)
   ______
4. The Arctic / Iceland (cold)
   ______
5. Sharks / dolphins (dangerous)
   ______
6. Hawaii / Alaska (warm)
   ______
7. Hotels / youth hostels (expensive)
   ______

Total: 6

Superlatives

4 Write sentences in the superlative.

1. Russia / big / country / in the world
   Russia is the biggest country in the world.
2. The cheetah / fast / animal in the world
   ______
3. The *Mona Lisa* / famous / painting in the world
   ______
4. The University of Al-Karaouine in Morocco / old / university in the world
   ______
5. The Himalayas / high / mountains in the world
   ______
6. The Australian box jellyfish / poisonous / creature in the world
   ______

Total: 5

should/shouldn't

5 Complete the sentences with *should* or *shouldn't* and the verb.

1 It's a good idea to get up early.
You *should get* up early.
2 I suggest you tell him what you think.
You ___________ him what you think.
3 It isn't a good idea to drink your tea with so much honey.
You ___________ your tea with so much honey.
We ___________ sandwiches in the classroom.
4 It isn't a good idea to talk and eat at the same time.
You ___________ ___________ at the same time.
5 It isn't OK to talk in the library.
You ___________ quiet in the library.

Total: 4

Language builder

6 Complete the conversation with the missing words. Circle the correct options.

Dear Becky,
We [1]___________ a wonderful time on our holiday in Australia. We [2]___________ at a beautiful beach hotel. It's [3]___________ than at home! I love [4]___________ in the ocean. We [5]___________ snorkelling near the beach yesterday when we saw [6]___________ dolphins! I think they're [7]___________ sea creatures in the world! I took [8]___________ of pictures! I'll send you some photos. It's really important to be careful in the sun over here. They told us we [9]___________ wear hats all the time and we [10]___________ out in the middle of the day.
See you soon!
Angie

	a	b	c
1	have	(b) 're having	do have
2	stay	're staying	stayed
3	sunny	sunniest	sunnier
4	swim	swimming	swam
5	was	were	are
6	much	any	some
7	the beautiful	the most beautiful	the more beautiful
8	a lot	some	many
9	should	aren't	shouldn't
10	aren't going	should go	shouldn't go

Total: 9

Vocabulary builder

7 Choose the correct word.

1 My uncle's daughter is my *cousin*.
a aunt b cousin c mother
2 We studied the rivers of France in ___________ today.
a Geography b History c Maths
3 Your bedroom is really ___________. Pick up all those things!
a unfriendly b unfair c untidy
4 He ran very fast, but he couldn't ___________ them.
a climb b chase c catch
5 Is there any ice cream in the ___________?
a cooker b freezer c fridge
6 He plays the piano and the guitar. He's an amazing ___________.
a dancer b scientist c musician
7 I think there are some biscuits in the ___________.
a cupboard b wardrobe c sink
8 Where's the ___________? I'm going to lie down on the sofa.
a carpet b blanket c towel
9 We're ___________ in the park at the moment. Do you want to come?
a walk b walking c doing
10 The sun ___________ before breakfast.
a put up b went up c came up

Total: 9

Speaking

8 Circle the correct options.

Mum: Tom, [1]**(will) / shall** you help me in the kitchen?
Tom: OK. [2]**Do / Shall** I make the salad?
Mum: Yes, please. [3]**Will / Shall** you also do me a favour and take the dog out for a walk after dinner?
Tom: Sorry, I [4]**can't / don't**. I need to finish my homework. [5]**I'll / I** ask Sue.
Mum: That's OK. [6]**I'll / Shall I** do it.
Tom: [7]**Shall / Can** I tell Sue and Dad it's time for dinner?
Mum: Yes, please.

Total: 6

Total: 57

Get it right! Unit 3

Comparatives and superlatives

Remember that:

- with short adjectives we add ***-er*** or ***-est***.
- with long adjectives we use ***more*** or ***the most***.

1 Find and correct five more mistakes with comparatives and superlatives.

Louisa: What do you think of my new bedroom? It's ~~more bigger~~ *bigger* than my old room.
Izzie: It's great! I love the big windows. It's more lighter than your old room too.
Louisa: Yes. And I've got some new furniture. Do you like it?
Izzie: Yes, it's moderner, isn't it? The old stuff was … well, more traditional.
Louisa: I know, it was awful! I had the most old wardrobe in the world!
Izzie: This one's much more nicer. You've got loads of space for all your clothes.
Louisa: And come look at the view from the window. It's the beautifullest view in town.

should/shouldn't

Remember, we use the infinitive without ***to*** after ***should*** and ***shouldn't***.

✓ *You **should avoid** watching TV.*
✗ ~~*You should to avoid watching TV.*~~
✓ *You **shouldn't eat** a big meal before going to bed.*
✗ ~~*You mustn't eating a big meal before going to bed.*~~

2 Are the sentences correct? Correct the incorrect sentences.

Six tips for a successful exam

1 You should ~~to~~ make a timetable of all the work you need to do.
2 You should getting at least 8 hours of sleep every night.
3 You shouldn't work late in the evening.
4 You should to remember to take a break.
5 You should going for a walk every day.
6 You shouldn't forget to eat!
7 You should to drink a lot of water.

Prepositions of place

Remember that:

- we use ***in*** with rooms, towns and countries.
  ✓ *Maisie lives **in** the USA.*
- we use ***on*** with surfaces, e.g. *floor, wall, table.*
  ✓ *There is a computer **on** my desk.*
- we usually use ***at*** with buildings, e.g. *school, home.*
  ✓ *We stayed **at** a very unusual hotel.*

3 Complete the sentences with *at, in* or *on*.

1 *In* the kitchen, there's a fridge, a cooker and a dishwasher.
2 There is a library at school, but I prefer to do my homework ______ home.
3 I like the picture ______ the wall in the bedroom.
4 When it's cold, I put a blanket ______ the bed.
5 There's a lamp ______ the table in the living room.
6 I bought a beautiful mirror ______ San Francisco.

Spell it right! Comparative adjectives

Remember that:

- with short adjectives (one syllable) ending in vowel + consonant, we double the final consonant and add ***-er*** to form the comparative.
  His bedroom is big. → *His bedroom is **bigger** than mine.*
- we do not use ***more*** or ***very*** before comparative adjectives ending in ***-er***.
  ✓ *His bedroom is **bigger** than mine.*
  ✗ ~~*His bedroom is more bigger than mine.*~~
  ✗ ~~*His bedroom is very bigger than mine.*~~
- with long adjectives (two syllables +) we use ***more*** before the adjective.
  Their house is beautiful. → *Their house is **more** beautiful than ours.*
- with adjectives that have two syllables and end in *-y*, we remove the *-y* and add ***-ier***.
  Your garden is pretty. → *Your garden is **prettier** than ours.*

4 Write the comparative forms of the adjectives.

1 cold *colder*
2 expensive ______
3 tidy ______
4 comfortable ______
5 small ______
6 relaxing ______
7 high ______
8 easy ______

4 A balancing act

General and specific competences from the curriculum explored in the unit

1. Understand oral messages in different communication situations
1.1. Identify essential information from the news presented on TV/recorded materials related to different events, when the comment is illustrated by pictures
1.2. Identify details from messages and interactions on predictable topics, when the speakers/interlocutors talk clearly and slowly
1.3. Identify specific aspects of the culture of the language studied

2. Speak in different communication situations
2.1. Present plans, intentions and future projects
2.2. Give a short and simple presentation on activities
2.3. Initiate, continue and finish a dialogue on familiar or personal interest topics
2.4. Participate in conversations related to planning activities
2.5. Show interest in participating in a verbal exchange

3. Understand written messages in different communication situations
3.1. Select necessary information from lists or simple functional texts (brochures, menus, schedules, ads)
3.2. Extract information from multiple short texts based on several predefined or negotiated criteria/constraints
3.3. Identify information from a simple written letter/email to write an answer
3.4. Show willingness to be informed through reading

4. Write messages in everyday communication situations
4.1. Complete a form with personally identifiable information (education, interests, competences)
4.2. Write a very simple personal letter (digital version included) to express thanks or apologies
4.3. Tell a story, in short, using linkers to emphasise the chronological order
4.4. Write simple and coherent texts on specific topics of interest
4.5. Participate in the exchange of written messages

Competenţele generale și specifice din programa școlară, urmărite în unitatea de învăţare

1. Receptarea de mesaje orale în diverse situaţii de comunicare
1.1. Identificarea informaţiilor esențiale din știrile prezentate la TV/materiale înregistrate, referitoare la diferite evenimente, atunci când comentariul este ilustrat prin imagini
1.2. Identificarea detaliilor din mesaje și interacţiuni pe subiecte previzibile când locutorii/interlocutorii vorbesc clar și rar
1.3. Identificarea unor elemente culturale specifice limbii studiate

2. Exprimarea orală în diverse situaţii de comunicare
2.1. Prezentarea unor planuri/unor intenţii și proiecte de viitor
2.2. Descrierea scurtă, elementară a unor activități
2.3. Inițierea, susținerea și încheierea unui dialog pe teme familiare sau de interes personal
2.4. Participarea la conversaţii în legătură cu planificarea unor activităţi
2.5. Manifestarea interesului pentru participarea la schimbul verbal

3. Receptarea de mesaje scrise în diverse situaţii de comunicare
3.1. Extragerea informaţiilor necesare din liste sau din texte funcţionale simple (pliante, meniuri, orare, reclame)
3.2. Extragerea informațiilor din mai multe texte scurte pe baza mai multor criterii/constrângeri prestabilite sau negociate
3.3. Identificarea informaţiilor dintr-o scrisoare personală simplă/e-mail în vederea redactării unui răspuns
3.4. Manifestarea disponibilităţii pentru informare prin lectură

4. Redactarea de mesaje în diverse situaţii de comunicare
4.1. Completarea unui formular cu informaţii de identificare (educaţie, interese, competenţe)
4.2. Redactarea unei scrisori personale (inclusiv digitale) foarte simple exprimând mulțumiri sau scuze
4.3. Relatarea pe scurt a unei întâmplări utilizând cuvinte de legătură pentru a marca ordinea cronologică
4.4. Redactarea de texte simple și coerente pe teme de interes
4.5. Participarea la schimbul de mesaje scrise

4 A balancing act

Vocabulary

Priorities

1 ★ **Complete the word puzzle with the clues. What is the mystery word?**

1		*s*	*p*	*o*	*r*	*t*	*s*			
2										
3										
4										
5										
6										
7										
8										

1 My friend Matt loves doing ___*sports*___. He plays football, volleyball and tennis.
2 I go to bed after midnight so I don't get enough ______________.
3 My Mum always says 'With work and family I never have ______________ by myself'.
4 I spend a lot of time on the internet chatting with my friends ______________.
5 My friend Alex draws comics. She loves doing ______________ things.
6 Clara loves going to the shopping mall to ______________ out with friends.
7 We're going to shop for ______________ on Saturday.
8 Everyone helps ______________ the house at the weekend. I hate it!

Mystery word: These are all activities that a ______________ does.

2 ★ **Match the verbs with the nouns.**

1 competing in — e
2 hang out
3 doing
4 getting
5 having
6 helping

a time by yourself
b around the house
c something creative
d enough sleep
e sports events
f with friends

3 ★★ **Complete the text with words from Exercises 1 and 2.**

I come from a large family. It's not easy! We all take turns [1] *helping around the house*, like washing the floor or cleaning the bathroom. I usually get my older sisters' dresses and jeans when they're too small for them, so I can only dream about [2] ______________________.

We've only got two computers too, so we don't [3] ______________________ very often. Also, [4] ______________________ is difficult – there's always something happening with the family. And [5] ______________ is a problem, because when we go to bed my sisters and I sometimes talk for hours!

Of course I don't always go out with my big sisters, I [6] ______________________ of my own from school. My sisters and I all enjoy painting and drawing, too. [7] ______________ together is really nice. I also [8] ______________________. I do athletics and it's great when all my family come to support me! We're all very close!

4 ★★★ **What about you? Write at least five sentences about your priorities. Use vocabulary from Exercises 1 and 2. Explain how you spend your time in the week and at the weekend.**

I don't help around the house in the week, but on Saturday I do.

Language focus 1

should/must

1 ★ **Complete the rules in the table.**

1	In the affirmative, we use *should* + the ________.
2	We form negatives with ________ after *should*.
3	We form questions with *should* ________ the subject.
4	We use *should* to say we think something is a ________ idea.

2 ★ **Complete the text with *should* or *shouldn't*.**

My brother and I share a room and we're always fighting. He always says I [1] __should__ study more before my exams and I [2] ________ play computer games all the time. I tell him he [3] ________ leave his clothes on the floor, and that he [4] ________ go to bed earlier. Then he says I [5] ________ tell him what to do because he's older, and I say he [6] ________ have more respect. That's when Mum or Dad usually come in to say we [7] ________ stop shouting! [8] ________ we stop arguing all the time? I suppose so, but it's fun!

3 ★ **Circle the rules in the table.**

1	When we make the affirmative, negative and question with *must* and *should*, the grammar is **the same / different**.
2	We use the infinitive **with / without** *to* after *must* and *mustn't*.
3	We use *must* and *mustn't* to say we think something is **very / not important**.

4 ★★ **Complete the sentences with the correct form of *must* and the verbs in the box.**

> remember ~~see~~ leave help tell stay get up watch

1 You __must see__ these photos on my phone. They're great!
2 They ________ without us! Tell them to wait.
3 We ________ late on Saturday. We need to catch the bus at 9 o'clock.
4 ________ I ________ around the house now? I'm watching my favourite programme!
5 Joel ________ out late tonight. He's got an important match tomorrow.
6 Why ________ you ________ football all the time? I hate it!
7 You ________ me about your trip to Bogotá.
8 We ________ to text Jenny about the cinema.

5 ★★★ **Write sentences with *should/shouldn't* and *must/mustn't* and the words in brackets.**

1 It's very cold outside. (coat / catch)
You should wear a coat or you'll catch a cold.
2 I'm sometimes tired in my Maths class. (get / more sleep)
____
3 I never remember what homework I have to do. (concentrate)
____
4 I've got a really important exam tomorrow. (go to bed / late)
____
5 I usually get very hungry before lunch. (snack)
____
6 Olivia really wants me to help her. (call / her later)
____

Explore verb + noun collocations

6 ★★ **Match the sentence halves.**

1 Why are you watching — b
2 I'm hungry! I think I'll
3 You must get
4 I think I'm catching
5 We can't concentrate
6 Tom loves surfing

a in our lesson because there's too much noise.
b TV? Go outside and play!
c the internet, but he should go out more.
d more sleep! You look very tired.
e a cold. I don't feel well.
f have a snack.

Listening and vocabulary Adverbs of manner

Listening

1 ★★ **Listen to a radio programme discussing how teenagers spend their time. Tick (✓) the things in the list they talk about.**

a studying ✓
b helping around the house ☐
c social activities ☐
d after-school activities ☐
e holidays ☐
f homework ☐
g getting enough sleep ☐
h clothes and fashion ☐

2 ★★ **Listen again. Mark the sentences true *(T)* or false *(F)*.**

1 The discussion topic is what teenagers do at school. *F*
2 Jamie doesn't do any extra activities. ___
3 He usually feels tired. ___
4 The teacher thinks her students do too much. ___
5 She says students should meet every evening to do homework. ___
6 The parent agrees with the teacher. ___
7 He thinks teenagers should concentrate on schoolwork. ___
8 The psychologist agrees with the teenager. ___
9 She thinks being with friends is important. ___
10 She says that helping around the house and sleeping are both important. ___

Performing + Adverbs of manner

3 ★ **Complete the text with the words in the box.**

dancing	orchestra	act	voice	play the piano	~~on stage~~	microphone	instruments

The concert last night was amazing. The moment Jake came [1] *on stage* was magic. Everyone in the crowd started shouting, singing and [2] ______. There was a big [3] ______ behind the band and the sound was incredible. Jake took the [4] ______ and started singing 'Love is …'. He's got such a powerful [5] ______ and all the girls screamed! During the concert he played different [6] ______ and for the last song he sat down to [7] ______ on his own. And there was a surprise at the end – he told everyone he's going to [8] ______ in a film next month. He's a dream!

4 ★★★ **Use the words in Exercise 3 to make different words.**

1 We often make *microphone* shorter by seven letters. *mic*
2 Add *-al* to this word to describe a piece of music with no singing. ______
3 A person who dances. ______
4 A person who performs in a film or theatre. ______
5 Add *-l* to this word to describe music played by an orchestra. ______
6 A person who plays the piano. ______
7 Change this word to *voc-* and add *-al* and *-ist* for another word for a singer. ______
8 We also use this word as a verb to mean 'put on a performance'. ______

5 ★★ **Complete the sentences with the adverb form of the adjectives in brackets.**

1 We've learned the song *easily* (easy) because it's catchy.
2 Sam did his homework ______ (quick) because he wanted to play computer games.
3 We should talk ______ (quiet) because my sister's asleep.
4 My brother plays volleyball ______ (bad). He can't get the ball over the net!
5 This machine is difficult to use. Read the instructions ______ (careful).
6 She dresses ______ (beautiful).
7 They laughed very ______ (loud).
8 I thought he was treated very ______ (bad).

Language focus 2

(don't) have to

1 ★ **Complete the sentences in the box.**

With *have to* we use [1]________ or [2]________ to make negatives, and [3]________ or [4]________ to make questions.
After *have/has to* we use the [5]________ form of the verb.
Use *have/has to* to say that it is [6]________ to do something.
Use *don't / doesn't have to* to say that it is not [7]________ to do something, but that you [8]________ do it if you want.

2 ★ Circle **the correct form of *have to* in the sentences.**

Fashion ideas: *be yourself!*

1 It's essential to be yourself. Remember people **have to** / **don't have to** wear the same clothes as everyone else!

2 You **have to** / **don't have to** look for clothes or hairstyles which are a bit different.

3 There are a lot of cheap shops, so teenagers **have to** / **don't have to** spend a lot of money.

4 Everyone **has to** / **doesn't have to** experiment a little to find their own style.

5 At school we **have to** / **don't have to** be careful not to look too extreme!

6 You **have to** / **don't have to** follow fashion. If you don't like it, don't wear it!

3 ★★ **Complete the conversation between the PE teacher and a student with the correct form of *have to* and the word in brackets.**

A: [1] *Do I have to be* (I be) really fit to do a triathlon?
B: No, and [2]______________________________ (you be) very good at any of the individual sports.
A: [3]______________________________ (beginners swim) in open water, like a lake or the sea?
B: No, in all beginner races they swim in a pool.
A: [4]______________________________ (I wear) a helmet for the cycling part?
B: Yes, Every [5]______________________________ (cyclist wear) a helmet to compete.
A: Do I need a racing bicycle?
B: No, [6]______________________________ (your bicycle be) a special one.
A: What about the running part?
B: [7]______________________________ (every competitor wear) a microchip on their shoe, for their official time.
A: Right! Are the rules very complicated?
B: Yes, [8]______________________________ (you read) the rules carefully so you know what to do!

don't have to vs. *mustn't*

4 ★ **Complete the sentences with *don't have to* or *mustn't*.**

1 We *don't have to* sing if you don't want to.
2 You ______________ use your mobile phone while you're driving.
3 Today's Friday so I ______________ do my homework.
4 You ______________ forget to say good luck to Dad. He's got a concert tonight.
5 She ______________ use a microphone. I can hear her perfectly.
6 She ______________ be late for the concert or they won't let her in.

Explore prepositions

5 ★★ Circle **the correct words.**

1 There's a cinema **in front of** / **above** my uncle's house. You can see it through the window.
2 Don't come in the house **over** / **until** I tell you to.
3 I try to balance my time **between** / **near** athletics and homework.
4 We've got a big park **inside** / **behind** my house.
5 My school is **near** / **until** our house so I walk to school every day.
6 The party was full **of** / **over** kids from his school.
7 You must be **until** / **over** 18 to watch this film.
8 Let's see who's taller. Stand **outside** / **beside** me and we can see.

6 ★★★ **Imagine you are a rich and famous person. How is your imaginary life different from your real life? Write in your notebook at least five sentences about things you *have to* do now and things you *don't have to* do.**

I'm a film star! I don't have to make my bed ...

Reading

1 ★ **Read about the problems a teenage athlete has. Complete the text with the headings in the box.**

Diet   Schoolwork   ~~The attitude of my friends~~   Getting enough sleep

BEING A TEENAGE ATHLETE

JUGGLING MY LIFE!

HOME   ABOUT   BLOG   CONTACT

I'm a long-jumper. I train four times a week and compete on Sundays. I love athletics, but my life isn't easy and involves a lot of ***juggling***. Schoolwork, training, family life, sleeping, and socialising all need my attention and there are only 24 hours in a day! So what are my biggest problems?

1 *The attitude of my friends*: Most of my friends aren't ***sporty*** so they don't understand why I am. If we're hanging out and I have to leave early because I've got an ***athletics meeting*** on the next day, they say, 'No, Sam, you mustn't go!'

2 ______________________: An athlete can eat a lot and not get fat, but I must eat healthy food to support all the exercise (and ***brainwork***!) I do. I have to ignore the machines selling sweets and chocolate (not easy!) and make sure I eat enormous ***helpings*** of protein, vegetables, and fruit.

3 ______________________: When I'm training hard I should go to bed early, or I quickly feel exhausted.

This is a problem, as I've sometimes got ***loads of*** homework to do when I get home. Luckily, there's Saturday!

4 ______________________: I have to use every free moment. I often ***revise*** in the car to and from training. I do homework after dinner, but I shouldn't stay up late, so usually I finish my coursework at the weekend, when my friends are out having fun. I'm not surprised they think I'm crazy!

I don't have to do this, so why do I? Because I'm good at it, and I want to win a gold medal!

2 ★★ **Complete the sentences with the words in the box. Use the words in *bold* in the text to help you.**

athletics meeting   revise   ~~loads of~~   helping (noun)   brainwork   ignore   juggling   sporty

1 Another phrase for *lots of* is *loads of*.
2 If you ______________ something, you act like it's not happening.
3 An ______________ is an event where people compete in sports like running or jumping.
4 If you like playing sports, you are a ______________ person.
5 A ______________ is a portion of food.
6 You have to think a lot when you do ______________.
7 To keep throwing three or four balls in the air, without dropping them, is called ______________.
8 To ______________ before an exam you read things you did in class and try to remember them.

3 ★★ **Choose the correct answers.**

1 How many times a week does Sam do athletics training?
   a five times a week
   (b) four times a week
2 Why can he eat a lot?
   a he does a lot of 'brainwork'
   b he doesn't get fat
3 What happens when he does a lot of training and he doesn't go to bed early?
   a he feels tired very quickly
   b he can't compete on Saturdays
4 How do Sam's friends feel about him?
   a they think he has fun
   b they think he's crazy

4 ★★★ **Write rules for Sam's life. Use *should/shouldn't, must/mustn't* and *has to/doesn't have to* and the words in the box.**

do homework   eat sweets and chocolate   go to parties   eat a lot of protein   stay up late   ~~train four times a week~~

1 *Sam has to train four times a week.*
2 ______________________________
3 ______________________________
4 ______________________________
5 ______________________________
6 ______________________________

Writing

A competition entry

1 Read Mike's competition entry. Did he enjoy the camp?

Write a review of an experience where you learned something new from using a computer. The best review will win a free video game!

Competition entry:

I love computer games, so I learned a lot from the two-week 'Game Design Summer Camp' I did this year. Everyone should try [1] *it* ! There were loads of [2] ______ to choose from. My [3] ______ were the talks by professional game designers and the gaming tournaments in the evenings and at weekends. And every afternoon we had outdoor activities, like swimming and volleyball. But the most important [4] ______ was designing a 3D video game. I did [5] ______ with my friends Carla and Sam – our instructors helped, of course! On the last day, when we finished our games, we had to present [6] ______ to a group of experts.

I was terrified, but [7] ______ were really nice. What did I learn? I learned how computer games work and I also learned how to do a good presentation. Not bad!

Mike

2 Read the competition entry again and match the questions with the answers.

1 What was the camp about? *c*
2 When was it? ___
3 How did Mike learn about computer games? ___
4 What did they do in the evenings and at weekends? ___
5 What activities were there in the afternoon? ___
6 Who did he design a game with? ___
7 What did they do at the end of the course? ___
8 What did Mike think of the course? ___

a His friends Carla and Sam.
b There was information from professionals.
c How to design computer games.
d In the summer.
e They presented their game to experts.
f It was amazing.
g Sports and outdoor activities.
h Compete in computer games.

Useful language Avoiding repetition

3 Complete Mike's competition entry with the words in the box.

~~it~~	this	activities	favourites	one	them	they

4 Rewrite the sentences to avoid repetition. Use the text in Exercise 1 to help you.

1 I went to an amazing summer camp. The camp was about performing and acting.
I went to an amazing summer camp. It was about performing and acting.

2 There were lots of activities, but my favourite activities were juggling and singing.
______

3 I sang a song and then my friend sang a song by BTS.
______

4 We tried juggling, but juggling is really difficult.
______

5 There were big helpings of vegetables, but I didn't eat the helpings of vegetables.
______

6 All the students on the camp were the same age as me and all the students were really good actors.
______

Writing

5 Complete the sentences with the correct prepositions.

1 There were loads ___of___ activities to try.
2 We had a chance to hang out ____________ people from different countries.
3 Sailing camp was perfect ____________ me.
4 You choose ____________ six activities.
5 At night, we sat ____________ a fire singing.
6 We went into town to shop ____________ souvenirs.

> **WRITING TIP**
> Make it better! ✓✓✓
> Use time expressions, but be careful with articles and prepositions.

6 Choose the correct time expressions.

1 We played basketball **in / in the** afternoons. (in the circled)
2 There were different activities **at / in the** night.
3 Most people went home **in / at** weekends.
4 The activities finished **at / to** 4 o'clock.
5 **On / In** the first day, we got into groups.
6 They put on films **at every night / every night**.

> **WRITING TIP**
> Make it better! ✓✓✓
> Use transition words to join sentences and ideas.

7 Complete the competition entry with the words in the box.

of course	And then	Actually
~~In fact~~	So far	For instance

> Before I went to surf camp last summer, I didn't like the sea. 1 ___In fact___, I hated it! However, the camp was amazing and, 2 ____________, I had a great time. There were lots of activities. 3 ____________, you could try windsurfing or kitesurfing. 4 ____________ if you didn't want to go in the water, you could learn about surfboards. 5 ____________ surfboards are difficult to take care of. 6 ____________, it's the best camp I've been on.

8 Read the competition entry again. Tick (✓) the things in the list that Mike writes about.

- the daytime/night/weekend activities ☐
- the instructors / other campers ☐
- the daily routine ☐
- why you liked it ☐
- the food ☐
- the weather ☐

PLAN

9 Read about the competition in the box. Use the headings in Exercise 8 or your own ideas to make notes.

> **ACTIVITY CAMP COMPETITION**
>
> **Win a *FREE* activity camp for two weeks!**
>
> Write about an activity camp that you went to. What sort of camp was it? The best description will win two weeks at the best activity camp in the world!

WRITE

10 Write your competition entry. Look at page 55 of the Student's Book to help you.

CHECK

11 Check your writing. Can you say YES to these questions?

- Is there any repetition in your competition entry?
- Do you use transition words between ideas and sentences?
- Are the prepositions correct?
- Do you use time expressions correctly?
- Are the spelling and punctuation correct?

Do you need to write a second draft?

4 Review

Vocabulary

Priorities

1 Match the phrases with the examples.

1 chatting with friends online — b
2 hanging out with friends
3 shopping for clothes
4 helping around the house
5 getting enough sleep
6 having time for yourself
7 doing something creative
8 playing sports

a going to bed early
b using Facebook or Twitter to send messages to friends
c going to a café to be with your friends
d buying new shoes and jeans
e playing for your school basketball team
f reading a book in your room
g designing computer games
h cleaning your room and doing the washing-up

Total: 7

Performing

2 Put the letters in brackets in order to make words.

1 I can't hear you. Could you speak into the *microphone*? (poochminer)
2 To work on the radio, you have to have a nice __________. (icove).
3 He always gets very nervous before he goes on __________. (gsate).
4 Listening to an __________ live is amazing. (aeothsrcr)
5 We're going __________ on Friday. (gnadinc)
6 OK, you can sing and dance. But can you __________? (tca)
7 She played all the __________ on her last album. (rutsmnetsin)
8 My grandmother plays the __________ and she's 85. (oniap)

Total: 7

Adverbs of manner

3 Put the letters in order to make adjectives. Change them to adverbs to complete each sentence.

1 1 She forgives *easily*. (syea)
2 I'm not surprised he failed his exam – he didn't exactly try very __________! (drha)
3 The accident was caused by people driving too __________ in bad conditions. (atsf)
4 She sings and plays the guitar quite __________. (dogo)
5 The teacher didnt't spell her name __________. (rrecotc)

Total: 4

Language focus

should/must

4 Complete the letters with *should* or *shouldn't*.

Dear Abby,
I have problems getting enough sleep. My parents say I [1] *should* go to bed earlier. My best friend told me I [2] ________ eat so much chocolate. My sister says I [3] ________ listen to relaxing music before I go to bed. What do you think? What [4] ________ I do?
'Worried'

Dear 'Worried',
There are many reasons for not getting enough sleep. You [5] ________ worry about it, because worrying can keep you awake. You also [6] ________ eat dinner late, and you [7] ________ try drinking some herbal tea before you go to bed.
Abby

Total: 6

5 Match the sentences and complete them with *must* or *mustn't*.

1 You look so tired. — e
2 You look hungry.
3 You're really late!
4 It's Mum's birthday tomorrow.
5 The concert is at 6 p.m.
6 I need to finish my Science project.

a You ________ eat some lunch.
b You ________ hurry!
c I ________ forget to buy her a card.
d We ________ be late.
e You *mustn't* go to bed late.
f I ________ do it this weekend.

Total: 5

(don't) have to vs. *mustn't*

6 Complete the sentences. Use *don't have to*, *doesn't have to* or *mustn't*.

1 At my school you *don't have to* wear a uniform.
2 Be careful, you __________ drop the glasses!
3 My brother is only four years old, so he __________ help around the house.
4 On Sundays, we get up early.
5 Tomorrow I have PE at school, so I __________ forget to bring my sports clothes.

Total: 4

Language builder

7 Circle the correct options.

Gina: What [1]___ last weekend?
Alex: I [2]___ my dog for a long walk. How about you?
Gina: I [3]___ a marathon. But when we [4]___, it [5]___ raining and we all got wet!
Alex: Oh, dear! [6]___ every day?
Gina: Before running a marathon, I [7]___ every morning.
Alex: Wow! You [8]___ tired sometimes. [9]___ eat a special diet?
Gina: Not really, I just eat lots of vegetables and fruit and I [10]___ eat sweets or chocolates. Do you want to go running with me?
Alex: OK. But first I [11]___ to find my running shoes!

1	(a) did you do	b you did do	c you did
2	a taked	b took	c take
3	a running	b runned	c ran
4	a were running	b ran	c run
5	a start	b was starting	c started
6	a Do you run	b You do run	c You run
7	a run usually	b usually running	c usually run
8	a must feel	b should feel	c did
9	a You have to	b You do have to	c Do you have to
10	a mustn't	b don't have to	c didn't eat
11	a must	b should	c have

Total: 10

Vocabulary builder

8 Circle the correct options.

1 It was cold, so the rain turned into ___.
(a) hail b thunder c heat wave

2 Sing into the ___. I can't hear you.
a piano b microphone c orchestra

3 It was -3 °C – the temperature was below ___.
a freezing b boiling c lightning

4 I study all the time. ___ is so important.
a Fashion b Education c Transport

5 When you cross the road you need to look ___ both directions.
a of b on c in

6 We need to take a ___ because it will be dark at night.
a compass b torch c camera

7 Pack a ___ because it can be cold at night.
a sleeping bag b water bottle c map

8 I like sports ___, like football and tennis matches.
a games b networks c events

9 I don't usually stay ___ late at the weekend.
a on b out c after

10 That new film is really scary – I was ___.
a terrified b stressed c exhausted

Total: 9

Speaking

9 Put the words in the correct order to make phrases for helping someone to do something.

1 show / Let / you / me
Let me show you.

2 know / you / to / it / how / Do / do / ?
______

3 good / very / at / not / I'm / Maths
______

4 hand / give / you / I'll / a / like / you / if
______

5 kind / really / That / 's
______

6 very / It / really / simple / 's
______

Total: 5

Total: 57

Get it right! Unit 4

should/must

Remember that:
- we use the infinitive without *to* after ***should/ shouldn't*** and ***must/mustn't***

  ✓ *You shouldn't go to bed late the night before an exam.*

  ✗ *You shouldn't ~~to~~ go to bed late the night before an exam.*

1 Find and correct five more mistakes with *should* and *must* in the rules.

IF THERE IS A FIRE IN YOUR HOME ...

1. You mustn't ~~to~~ panic! You should concentrate and breathe slowly.
2. You should to make sure everybody in the house is awake.
3. You must leave the house as quickly as possible.
4. If you can see smoke under the door, you mustn't to open it.
5. If the door is hot, you must to find another way to leave.
6. You should find a door that goes to the outside.
7. When you are out of the house, you must to telephone for help.
8. You shouldn't to go back into the house for any reason.

have to

Remember that:
- we don't usually use the contracted form of *have* with ***have to***

  ✓ *On Saturdays, I have to help with the shopping.*

  ✗ *On Saturdays, I've to help with the shopping.*
- we use the infinitive without *to* after *(don't) have to*

  ✓ *I have to look after my younger brother.*

  ✗ *I have to ~~looking~~ after my younger brother.*

  ✗ *I have to ~~looked~~ after my younger brother.*
- we use *have* after *I/you/we/they*, and *has* after *he/ she/it*

  ✓ *My grandmother has to go to the hospital.*

  ✗ *My grandmother ~~have~~ to go to the hospital.*

2 Find and correct six more mistakes with *have to* in the email.

YourMAIL | New | Reply | Delete | Junk

Hi Lucy,

I'm sorry I can't hang out with you tomorrow. ~~I've~~ *I have* to do so many things before school starts again on Monday! Tomorrow morning I have to going shopping for new shoes for school. Then, I have to took my brother to the dentist. He have to be there at 12 o'clock. My mum can't take him because she have to work. This afternoon I've to help around the house because my grandparents are coming to visit. I have to spent all weekend with them! I don't really mind, but I never have any time by myself!

I have to go now.

Bye!

Claire

need to

- we use the infinitive with ***to*** after ***need***

  ✓ *I need to be alone sometimes.*

  ✗ *I ~~need be~~ alone sometimes.*

  ✗ *I ~~need being~~ alone sometimes.*

3 Circle the correct option.

1. There are three things you need **remember / to remember** for the exam.
2. To get to sleep, you need **to feel / feeling** relaxed.
3. You really need **catch / to catch** up on your sleep. You're studying too hard.
4. You need **doing / to do** more exercise.
5. Teenagers need **to get / get** at least eight hours of sleep every night.
6. I need **to help / helping** my dad tomorrow.

5 Visions of the future

General and specific competences from the curriculum explored in the unit

1. Understand oral messages in different communication situations
1.1. Identify essential information from the news presented on TV/recorded materials related to different events, when the comment is illustrated by pictures
1.2. Identify details from messages and interactions on predictable topics, when the speakers/interlocutors talk clearly and slowly
1.3. Identify specific aspects of the culture of the language studied

2. Speak in different communication situations
2.1. Present plans, intentions and future projects
2.2. Give a short and simple presentation on activities
2.3. Initiate, continue and finish a dialogue on familiar or personal interest topics
2.4. Participate in conversations related to planning activities
2.5. Show interest in participating in a verbal exchange

3. Understand written messages in different communication situations
3.1. Select necessary information from lists or simple functional texts (brochures, menus, schedules, ads)
3.2. Extract information from multiple short texts based on several predefined or negotiated criteria/constraints
3.3. Identify information from a simple written letter/email to write an answer
3.4. Show willingness to be informed through reading

4. Write messages in everyday communication situations
4.1. Complete a form with personally identifiable information (education, interests, competences)
4.2. Write a very simple personal letter (digital version included) to express thanks or apologies
4.3. Tell a story, in short, using linkers to emphasise the chronological order
4.4. Write simple and coherent texts on specific topics of interest
4.5. Participate in the exchange of written messages

Competenţele generale şi specifice din programa şcolară, urmărite în unitatea de învăţare

1. Receptarea de mesaje orale în diverse situaţii de comunicare
1.1. Identificarea informaţiilor esenţiale din ştirile prezentate la TV/materiale înregistrate, referitoare la diferite evenimente, atunci când comentariul este ilustrat prin imagini
1.2. Identificarea detaliilor din mesaje şi interacţiuni pe subiecte previzibile când locutorii/interlocutorii vorbesc clar şi rar
1.3. Identificarea unor elemente culturale specifice limbii studiate

2. Exprimarea orală în diverse situaţii de comunicare
2.1. Prezentarea unor planuri/unor intenţii şi proiecte de viitor
2.2. Descrierea scurtă, elementară a unor activităţi
2.3. Iniţierea, susţinerea şi încheierea unui dialog pe teme familiare sau de interes personal
2.4. Participarea la conversaţii în legătură cu planificarea unor activităţi
2.5. Manifestarea interesului pentru participarea la schimbul verbal

3. Receptarea de mesaje scrise în diverse situaţii de comunicare
3.1. Extragerea informaţiilor necesare din liste sau din texte funcţionale simple (pliante, meniuri, orare, reclame)
3.2. Extragerea informaţiilor din mai multe texte scurte pe baza mai multor criterii/constrângeri prestabilite sau negociate
3.3. Identificarea informaţiilor dintr-o scrisoare personală simplă/e-mail în vederea redactării unui răspuns
3.4. Manifestarea disponibilităţii pentru informare prin lectură

4. Redactarea de mesaje în diverse situaţii de comunicare
4.1. Completarea unui formular cu informaţii de identificare (educaţie, interese, competenţe)
4.2. Redactarea unei scrisori personale (inclusiv digitale) foarte simple exprimând mulţumiri sau scuze
4.3. Relatarea pe scurt a unei întâmplări utilizând cuvinte de legătură pentru a marca ordinea cronologică
4.4. Redactarea de texte simple şi coerente pe teme de interes
4.5. Participarea la schimbul de mesaje scrise

5 Visions of the future

Vocabulary

Computer words

1 ★ Use the pictures to find eight more computer words in the word search.

1 
2 
3 
4 
5 
6 
7 
8 
9 

m	e	m	o	r	y	s	t	i	c	k	p
i	t	o	u	c	h	s	c	r	e	e	n
c	i	u	e	e	c	v	w	h	p	y	e
r	m	s	f	h	k	o	p	e	h	b	x
o	o	e	c	h	p	l	a	p	t	o	p
c	r	o	j	m	e	t	p	u	h	a	r
h	g	a	t	m	l	o	p	t	b	r	i
i	n	b	u	r	w	b	u	k	u	d	n
p	a	s	g	h	t	t	a	b	l	e	t
q	o	s	m	a	r	t	p	h	o	n	e
p	r	b	u	i	e	s	c	m	u	e	r

2 ★★ Complete the sentences with the words from Exercise 1.

1 I lost my *memory stick* with our school project on it, but later I found it in my jeans pocket.
2 It's easier to write emails using a ___________ than on a touchscreen.
3 Now most phones have a ___________ without buttons. You put your finger on the icons instead.
4 My mum hasn't got a ___________ because she only uses a phone to make calls.
5 I like my ___________ because the touchscreen is bigger than on a smartphone.
6 Our ___________ can scan things and make photocopies too. It's amazing.
7 I take my ___________ on holiday because my computer is too heavy and I haven't got a tablet.
8 You don't need a ___________ with a tablet.
9 Without a ___________, computers, laptops and tablets don't work.

3 ★★★ Jack has got five of the things from Exercise 1. Read what he says and complete the table.

1 I've got one of these. It's bigger than a tablet, but I can use it to do more things.
2 I haven't got one of these, but my father has. He loves it because it's much smaller than a laptop!
3 Of course I've got one of these – a new one with a really good camera. I made my first call on it yesterday!
4 I had one of these, but it broke. I don't miss it because I don't usually print anything anyway.
5 I've got one of these. It's really useful because you can use it on any computer, but I think it's full because I've got a lot of photos on it!
6 Yes, I've also got one of these little things. It's from an old computer.

Jack has got …	Jack hasn't got …
a laptop	

4 ★★★ Which of these things do you and your friends use? When do you use them? Write about five of them.

memory stick   mouse   laptop   touchscreen   tablet   printer   smartphone

Most of my friends use a memory stick to put school projects and other homework on. We can take them home and back to school to show to other people.

Language focus 1

will/*won't*

1 ★ Complete the rules in the grammar table.

1	We use *will* and *won't* for predictions / intentions.
2	We use *will* / *won't* + infinitive without *to* / infinitive with *to*.
3	We form the question with *will* / *do* + subject + *will* / infinitive.

2 ★ Complete the predictions about the future. Use the verbs in the box.

be (x2) celebrate find go live need study use

1 Children *won't go* (✗) to school every day. They ___________ (✓) at home, on their computers.
2 People ___________ (✓) longer. Most people ___________ (✓) their hundredth birthday.
3 Cars ___________ (✗) a driver anymore. They ___________ (✓) a computer to drive.
4 Scientists ___________ (✓) life on other planets.
5 The weather ___________ (✗) how it is now. There ___________ (✓) a big climate change.

3 ★★ Put the words in the correct order to make interview questions.

Adnan, you're a millionaire at the age of 18.

1 with the money / you / What / will / do / ?
What will you do with the money?
2 type / will / car / What / you / of / buy / ?
____
3 trophies / any / Will / your team / win / this season / ?
____
4 How / score / goals / will / many / you / this season / ?
____
5 you / will / Where / be / ten years from now / ?
____

4 ★★ Complete the sentences with *will/won't* and the verbs in brackets. Then match them with the questions in Exercise 3.

a I hope I*'ll be* married and I ___________ lots of kids. I love kids! (be, have) *5*
b I think I ___________ more than last year. (score) ___
c I'm sure I ___________ a car and a house, but I probably ___________ it all. I ___________ some for the future. (buy, not spend, save) ___
d Of course we ___________! I think this team ___________ the league and the cup! (win, win) ___
e I probably ___________ a sports car. I ___________ before I pass my driving test! (get, decide) ___

5 ★★★ Complete the predictions of the food scientist with *will/won't* and the verbs in brackets.

I think our food [1] *will taste* (taste) the same but we definitely [2] ___________ (not produce) it the same way. Producing meat is very expensive so we [3] ___________ (not eat) animal meat in the future – I'm sure. In fact, scientists [4] ___________ (produce) our meat. People [5] ___________ (find) new things to eat so we [6] ___________ (catch) different types of fish but I don't think people in Europe [7] ___________ (eat) insects. I think we [8] ___________ definitely ___________ (eat) less meat than we do now.

Explore suffixes *-ful* and *-less*

6 ★★ Complete the definitions with the words in the box.

beautiful useless wonderful painful ~~careless~~ hopeless

1 A person who does not look after their things is *careless*.
2 When a part of your body hurts, it is ___________.
3 A situation is ___________ when there is nothing you can do to make it better.
4 Something is ___________ when it doesn't work or it doesn't do what you need it do to.
5 ___________ things or people look good.
6 ___________ means very good.

Listening and vocabulary

Technology verbs + prepositions

1 ★ **Match the verbs in the box with the definitions.**

click on	sign in	scroll down	shut down
~~turn down~~	turn on	turn up	log on

1 make something quieter *turn down*
2 move a web page while you're reading ______
3 start a machine ______
4 choose something on the screen ______
5 turn off a computer ______
6 make something louder ______
7 enter a password to start your computer ______
8 enter a password to read your emails or see an online account ______

2 ★★ **Complete the text with the correct form of the verbs from Exercise 1.**

Mum: Where's that video you were telling me about?
Liam: Let's see. Yes, that's the page. Now [1]*scroll down* to the bottom and then [2]______ the link that says 'Summer camp video'.
Mum: Great. Thanks.
Liam: I'm going to bed. Don't forget to [3]______ the computer when you finish.
Mum: Liam, can you [4]______ the music, please? It's very loud.
Liam: Oh, Mum!
Mum: Actually, you should stop the music – it's late and you have to go to bed.
Liam: But Mum! I just [5]______ it ______ five minutes ago!

Listening

3 ★ **Listen to Mark talking to Liz about a programme he watched on TV. What was the programme about? Who talks about the things in the pictures?**

1 remote control

2 fingerprint

3 standby

4 power cut

4 ★★ **Listen again and circle the correct options.**

1 Mark watched a **TV programme / film** about smarthomes.
2 You **can / can't** control everything in your house when you're not at home.
3 Bill Gates spent $100,000,000 on his **TV / smarthome**.
4 The lights turn **off / on** automatically when you walk into a room.
5 You can turn on the bathroom shower from the **living room / bedroom**.
6 You **need / don't need** a key to get into your smarthome.
7 Liz's ideal home is as **simple / beautiful** as possible.

Language focus 2

Question tags

1 ★ **Circle the correct words in the grammar table.**

1	Question tags are short questions that we add at the **beginning / end** of a sentence in spoken English and sometimes in informal writing.
2	We can use them to ask for **agreement / opinions**.
3	We add a negative tag after a positive **sentence / question** or a positive tag after a **positive / negative** sentence.

2 ★★ **Match the sentence beginnings (1–6) with the sentence endings (a–f).**

1 We've got a test next week, ... *b*
2 She forgot to give us the link to her blog, ... ___
3 Studying will be more fun with tablets, ... ___
4 You lost your memory stick again, ... ___
5 He should buy a new phone, ... ___
6 The computer software is updating again, ... ___

a isn't it?
b haven't we?
c won't it?
d didn't she?
e shouldn't he?
f didn't you?

3 ★★ **Complete the sentences with the correct question tags.**

1 Students should always do their homework, *shouldn't they*?
2 The teacher isn't coming today, ______________?
3 Laptops are cheaper when you buy them online, ______________?
4 You have to finish your science project tonight, ______________?
5 You remembered to turn the computer off, ______________?
6 The neighbours are always angry when he turns the music up, ______________?
7 We can't take the bus home at this hour, ______________?
8 The concert was great, ______________?

4 ★★★ **Write question tags matching the sentence halves. Use the correct form of the verbs.**

1 We / go to the cinema / this weekend
2 The touchscreen / not work
3 You / should / turn off / the TV
4 He / always / listen / to music / loudly
5 We / have to / buy / the tickets soon

a should not / you?
b do not / we?
c be not / we?
d do not / he?
e it / be?

1 *We're going to the cinema this weekend, aren't we?*
2 ______________
3 ______________
4 ______________
5 ______________

Explore phrasal verbs 1

5 ★★ **Complete the text with the correct form of the phrasal verbs in the box.**

take off   put on   sit down   ~~get up~~   look for

Carl [1] *got up* early again. He [2] ______ at his desk. What a mess! He [3] ______ his glasses, but he couldn't find them. He pushed some papers and they fell on the floor. His glasses were under the papers. He [4] ______ them ______ and turned up the music. He tried to work, but he was tired. He [5] ______ his glasses, threw them on the desk and went to sleep.

Reading

1 ★ **Read the text about cars in the future. How are they different from the cars we have now?**

WHERE'S THE DRIVER? »»

Imagine going into town to go shopping. You arrive at the station. The shopping centre is a 20-minute walk away, but you have a better idea. You get in a pod – a small car. You can't drive, but that's no problem, because the pod doesn't need a driver. It has a computer! There's a screen, so you surf the web or play computer games. Is this science fiction? No, it will soon be reality.

A hundred driverless pods will soon be on the road in the British town of Milton Keynes. They will travel on the pavement, but their special computer program will use GPS, HD cameras and sensors to navigate safely. Each pod can carry two people and travel at a maximum speed of about 19 kph. They save time and are better for the environment, because they don't cause pollution.

In 2015, Waymo LLC, formerly known as the Google Self-Driving Car Project, provided the world's first 'self-driving car' on public roads. The US states of Nevada, Florida and California permit driverless cars on normal roads with other traffic. In October 2020, Waymo became the first company to offer self-driving taxi rides without safety drivers in the vehicle.

So, in the future we will probably have the opportunity to download an app onto your smartphone and call a driverless pod to take you where you want to go. Another option, of course, is to walk!

2 ★★ **Match the words from the text with their definitions.**

environment science fiction pollution ~~imagine~~ navigate

1 to picture something in your mind ___*imagine*___
2 a type of book or film usually about the future, space or other planets ______
3 move around something or find the right direction ______
4 the air, water and land on and in which people and animals live ______
5 something that happens when the air or water is not clean ______

3 ★★ **Read the text again. Mark the sentences *true (T)* or *false (F)*. Correct the false sentences.**

1 Driverless cars use a computer to drive the car. ___*T*___
2 If you can't drive, you can't go in a pod. ______
3 The pods in Milton Keynes will be on the road with other cars. ______
4 The pods won't go very fast. ______
5 Driverless cars won't help the environment. ______
6 Driverless cars can travel on the road in some parts of the US. ______
7 One day people will phone driverless taxis. ______

4 ★★★ **What do you think of driverless cars? Why are they a good idea? Can you think of any problems with them? Write four or five sentences.**

____
____
____
____
____

Writing

An opinion essay

1 **Read the question and the opinion essay. Does the writer agree or disagree with the question?**

How do you imagine your future? Will your life be very different from your parents'? Write an essay with the title: 'My life will be the same as my parents' lives. Do you agree?'

Give us your opinion.

Most people agree that nowadays life is very different from twenty years ago, so I don't think that my life will be exactly the same as my parents' lives. However, I don't think that it will be completely different.

For example, I'm sure that I will go to university, like my parents. I will try to look for a good job near where they live. It isn't as easy as it was, but I'm optimistic.

Some people say that the world is a smaller place because of the internet, while others believe that young people stay at home for longer. In my opinion, I'm more adventurous than my parents. When I finish university, I will probably work abroad for a while. My parents never did that! It would be interesting, wouldn't it?

In conclusion, I think I will have more opportunities than my parents, but it will probably be more difficult for me to find a secure job.

2 **Read the essay again. Tick (✓) the opinions from the essay.**

1 Life is different now from in the past. ☐
2 The writer's life will be the same as their parents' lives. ☐
3 It's not difficult to find a job. ☐
4 The internet changes how we see the world. ☐
5 There will be more possibilities in the future. ☐

Useful language Sequencing language 2

3 **Look back at the essay. Complete these phrases.**

1 *However*, I don't think
2 ________ my opinion,
3 ________ people say that
4 ________ people agree that
5 ________ believe that
6 ________ conclusion,
7 ________ example,
8 I'm ________ that

4 **Read the essay. Circle the correct options.**

[1]**Some people say that / Other people say that** the future will be better than the present. [2]**Some people say that / Other people say that** it will be worse, but [3]**most people agree that / in conclusion** it will be very different.
[4]**I'm sure that / Other people say that** my life will be very different in the future. [5]**However, / For example,** many things will be the same. [6]**In my opinion, / Most people agree that** my family and friends will always be important.
[7]**In conclusion, / However,** nobody knows what life will be like in the future. [8]**For example, / However,** isn't that exciting?

5 **Complete the sentences with the correct comparative or superlative form of the words in brackets.**

1 *The most important* (important) thing nowadays is to get a good education.
2 I think I'm ________ (adventurous) person in my family.
3 It's ________ (difficult) to find a job today than in the past.
4 We can find information much ________ (quick) than in the past.
5 I'm sure that people now aren't ________ (tall) than they were in the past.

Writing

UNIT 5

WRITING TIP

Make it better! ✓ ✓ ✓

We use sequencing language to organise our ideas in a text and help the reader understand the order in which the ideas / events are presented.

We use:

- *firstly* – to introduce an opening point;
- *secondly; thirdly* – to introduce another point;
- *however; but* – to show a contrast;
- *finally; lastly* – to introduce the final point;
- *in conclusion; to sum up* – to summarise an opinion.

6 Complete the text with the missing words.

Our lives will be very different in the future. One thing that will change is the way we buy things. [1]__________ we won't use real money anymore because it will disappear completely. We will use our mobile phones and our watches to pay for things. [2]__________ we will still have credit cards. [3]__________ we won't have to go to the supermarket to buy food. We will programme our fridges to order food for us online, [4]__________ we will still be able to go to shops and try on clothes when we want to. [5]__________ there will be no more banks. Everyone will go online to see how much money they have left and to pay bills. [6]__________ the future will bring many changes and it will get easier and easier to spend our money. We will have to be more careful!

WRITING TIP

Make it better! ✓ ✓ ✓

Explain your opinion: give reasons or examples.

I think life was difficult for my grandparents because they had to work very hard.

7 Look at the essay again. Find examples of when the writer gives reasons or examples for his/her opinion.

For example,

8 Tick (✓) the sentence that does not give reasons for the opinions.

1 We young people are more adventurous because we travel more than our parents did. ☐

2 Technology will help us. For example, the internet will give us more information. ☐

3 I'm optimistic about the future because I believe that the world will be a better place. ☐

4 We don't know what the world will be like in the future. ☐

5 Most people agree that life for young people is easier in some ways. For example, it is easier to study or go to university. ☐

9 Read the opinion essay again and order the paragraphs.

a arguments for the statement ___

b introduction and your opinion *1*

c conclusion and final opinion ___

d arguments against the statement ___

PLAN

10 You are going to write an opinion essay for the task in Exercise 1. Use the paragraphs in Exercise 9 and make notes.

WRITE

11 Write the opinion essay. Look at page 69 of the Student's Book to help you.

____

____

____

____

____

____

____

____

____

____

____

____

CHECK

12 Check your writing. Can you say YES to these questions?

- Did you use the essay structure in Exercise 9?
- Do you use comparative forms to compare your life to your parents' lives?
- Do you use *when* and *if* sentences correctly?
- Do you give reasons for and examples of your opinion?

Do you need to write a second draft?

5 Review

Vocabulary

Computer words

1 Circle the correct words.

A [1]**tablet / printer** is easy to carry. It has a [2]**touchscreen / smartphone** so you don't need a mouse or a [3]**keyboard / microphone.**

A [4]**laptop / tablet** is bigger and has a thin [5]**keyboard / memory stick**, a wireless [6]**mouse / microchip**, and a large [7]**smartphone / touchscreen**. You can use the [8]**keyboard / printer** to make copies.

Total: 7

Technology verbs + prepositions

2 Circle the correct options.

1 Sign **on to / in to** your account.
2 Log **up / on to** your computer.
3 Turn **on / over** the laptop.
4 Scroll **down / in** the web page.
5 Click **down / on** the icon.
6 Turn **in / up** the volume.
7 Shut **down / up** the computer when you finish.

Total: 6

Language focus

will/won't

3 Complete the text with *will* or *won't*.

What [1]___*will*___ our homes be like in the future? In the homes of the future, there [2]__________ be any housework to do, and there [3]__________ probably be any cooking because everyone [4]__________ have robot helpers to clean the house and cook the meals. The fridges [5]__________ connect to the internet and tell you what food to buy. The alarm clock [6]__________ read your daily schedule and know what time you need to get up for work. You [7]__________ drive to work, the car [8]__________ drive itself or we [9]__________ even have flying cars! I'm sure.

Total: 8

Question tags

4 Circle the correct options.

1 They **won't / don't** pass the exam, will they?
2 He doesn't know how to use a computer, **do / does** he?
3 We **aren't / won't** be allowed to use our smartphones in class, are we?
4 You can't swim all the way over there, **can / can't** you?
5 They will send you an email to inform you about your new job, **will / won't** they?
6 Mike should buy a new phone, **shouldn't / should** he?
7 He knows how to fix computers, **doesn't / does** he?

Total: 6

5 Complete the sentences with the correct question tags.

1 They have cheaper headphones in this shop, *don't they*?
2 Frank doesn't want to go to the party without Alison, __________?
3 Ben will post the photo on this blog this weekend, __________?
4 You forgot to phone your mum again, __________?
5 We could ask our teacher to give us the exam some other day, __________?

Total: 4

Writing

6 Write an opinion essay about how you imagine the future of transport. Write 60–80 words. Use as much of the language on page 66 as you can.

Total: 15

Total: 46

Language builder

7 Circle the correct options.

Martina: Is that a new smartphone?
Steve: Yes, it [1]__________. I [2]__________ it for my birthday and I [3]__________ how to use it.
Martina: Nice! And it has a lot of apps, doesn't it?
Steve: Yes, it does. But it hasn't got any games, [4]__________ it? I [5]__________ download some more.
Martina: Is it [6]__________ than your old phone?
Steve: Yes, but it [7]__________ as fast as those super-expensive ones.
Martina: My mum said she'll give me a smartphone. But I [8]__________ pass my exam first.
Steve: That's great! You [9]__________ like some of these new games.
Martina: Yes, but you know we [10]__________ use them at school.
Steve: Yes. The teacher said we [11]__________ use smartphones in the lesson.

1	**a** does	**(b)** is	**c** was
2	**a** get	**b** am getting	**c** got
3	**a** learn	**b** 'm learning	**c** will learn
4	**a** has	**b** does	**c** is
5	**a** should	**b** like	**c** prefer
6	**a** fast	**b** faster	**c** fastest
7	**a** is	**b** isn't	**c** doesn't
8	**a** have to	**b** will	**c** do
9	**a** do	**b** should	**c** will
10	**a** don't	**b** shouldn't	**c** won't
11	**a** must	**b** should	**c** mustn't

Total: 10

Vocabulary builder

8 Circle the correct options.

1 The police __________ the thieves down the street.
a jumped **(b)** chased **c** ran
2 We keep ice cream in the __________.
a dishwasher **b** freezer **c** microwave
3 Use the __________ to type your password.
a printer **b** mouse **c** keyboard
4 You can open the apps from the __________.
a keyboard **b** microchip **c** touchscreen
5 You can sit on a __________.
a sofa **b** wardrobe **c** curtain
6 The thief __________ into the bank through a window.
a climbed **b** caught **c** hid
7 You can cook spaghetti on the __________.
a fridge **b** cooker **c** heater
8 We were late so we ate our lunch __________.
a quickly **b** sleepily **c** slowly
9 I closed the __________ and went to bed.
a blanket **b** pillow **c** curtains
10 Scroll __________ the web page to see your emails.
a down **b** in **c** over
11 The road was icy so I walked very __________.
a easily **b** quickly **c** carefully

Total: 10

Speaking

9 Complete the conversation with the words in the box.

You have to …	How do I …	First	Now	~~work~~

Jenny: Is that a new tablet?
Sue: Yes! Do you want to try it?
Jenny: How does it [1] *work* ?
Sue: [2]________, you need to press the power button.
Jenny: OK. What do I do next?
Sue: [3]________, type in the password.
Jenny: [4]________ check my email?
Sue: [5]________ press the icon.
Jenny: I see! Thanks!

Total: 4

Total: 70

Get it right! Unit 5

will/won't

Remember, we use the infinitive without *to* after ***will*** and ***won't***.

✓ *Online friends **won't replace** real friends.*
✗ ~~*Online friends won't replaced real friends.*~~
✓ *The council **will** cars in the city centre.*
✗ ~~*The council will banned cars in the city centre.*~~

1 Correct four more mistakes in the conversation.

Juan: What are you going to do in the summer?
Marta: I think I'll ~~visited~~ ^visit my pen friend in Ireland. What about you?
Juan: I'll definitely travelled to Europe.
Marta: Oh, where will you go?
Juan: I'll probably flew to England, and study English there.
Marta: That's a great idea! Well, I'll saw you in London if I go there. That would be fantastic!

Question tags

Remember that:

- we use question tags at the end of a sentence in spoken English and sometimes in informal writing.
- we can use question tags to ask for agreement.
- we add a negative tag after a positive sentence or a positive tag after a negative sentence.
- we always put a comma before the tag.
- we never use tags after questions.

✓ He's such a nice person, isn't he?
✓ He isn't such a nice person, is he?
✗ ~~Is he a nice person, isn't he?~~

2 Are the question tags correct? Correct the incorrect ones.

1 You can come with me tomorrow, can you?
You can come with me tomorrow, can't you?
2 She lost her mobile phone didn't she?
____
3 Lucy would be very angry with me when she finds out, won't she?
____
4 Do you think it will be fun, do you?
____
5 You have to finish your homework, don't you?
____

Computer words

Remember that:

- we usually use ***the*** before *internet*.
  ✓ *I enjoy surfing **the** internet.*
- we use ***on***, not *in* or *with*, to talk about using the ***internet*** or a ***computer***.
  ✓ *I like playing **on my computer**.*
  ✗ ~~*I like playing with my computer.*~~
- we usually use ***a*** or ***the*** with ***computer***.
  ✓ *I want to learn how to use **a computer**.*
  ✗ ~~*I want to learn how to use computer.*~~
  ✓ *I really enjoy playing **on the computer**.*
  ✗ ~~*I really enjoy playing on computer.*~~

3 Find six more mistakes in the text.

I got ^a new computer for my birthday. I needed computer because I like using internet and playing games. Computer is useful for homework and there are lots of useful programs in the computer too. I've put the computer in my bedroom. When my friend visits me, we can play games with the computer. That's great, because he hasn't got computer at home.

Phrasal verbs

Remember that:

- we use ***on*** and ***off*** with ***take***, and ***down*** and ***up*** with ***turn*** for some meanings.
- we use ***on*** to talk about wearing something or making a piece of equipment start working.
  ✓ *He put **on** his coat and left the house.*
- we use ***off*** to talk about not wearing something or making a piece of equipment stop working.
  ✓ *You should take **off** your shoes when you go in.*
- we use ***down*** to talk about making something less, and ***up*** to talk about making something more.
  ✓ *You can turn **down** the music if it's too loud.*
  ✓ *You can turn **up** the music if it's too quiet.*

4 Add *on, off, down* or *up* to each sentence.

1 She turned ^on the TV to watch the news.
2 It was cold outside, so he put his hat.
3 Remember to turn the lights when you leave.
4 She took her coat because it was wet.
5 They turned the music because it was too loud.
6 Please turn the TV, it's not loud enough.

6 Life choices

General and specific competences from the curriculum explored in the unit

1. Understand oral messages in different communication situations
1.1. Identify essential information from the news presented on TV/recorded materials related to different events, when the comment is illustrated by pictures
1.2. Identify details from messages and interactions on predictable topics, when the speakers/interlocutors talk clearly and slowly
1.3. Identify specific aspects of the culture of the language studied

2. Speak in different communication situations
2.1. Present plans, intentions and future projects
2.2. Give a short and simple presentation on activities
2.3. Initiate, continue and finish a dialogue on familiar or personal interest topics
2.4. Participate in conversations related to planning activities
2.5. Show interest in participating in a verbal exchange

3. Understand written messages in different communication situations
3.1. Select necessary information from lists or simple functional texts (brochures, menus, schedules, ads)
3.2. Extract information from multiple short texts based on several predefined or negotiated criteria/constraints
3.3. Identify information from a simple written letter/email to write an answer
3.4. Show willingness to be informed through reading

4. Write messages in everyday communication situations
4.1. Complete a form with personally identifiable information (education, interests, competences)
4.2. Write a very simple personal letter (digital version included) to express thanks or apologies
4.3. Tell a story, in short, using linkers to emphasise the chronological order
4.4. Write simple and coherent texts on specific topics of interest
4.5. Participate in the exchange of written messages

Competenţele generale și specifice din programa școlară, urmărite în unitatea de învățare

1. Receptarea de mesaje orale în diverse situaţii de comunicare
1.1. Identificarea informaţiilor esențiale din știrile prezentate la TV/materiale înregistrate, referitoare la diferite evenimente, atunci când comentariul este ilustrat prin imagini
1.2. Identificarea detaliilor din mesaje și interacţiuni pe subiecte previzibile când locutorii/interlocutorii vorbesc clar și rar
1.3. Identificarea unor elemente culturale specifice limbii studiate

2. Exprimarea orală în diverse situaţii de comunicare
2.1. Prezentarea unor planuri/unor intenţii și proiecte de viitor
2.2. Descrierea scurtă, elementară a unor activități
2.3. Inițierea, susținerea și încheierea unui dialog pe teme familiare sau de interes personal
2.4. Participarea la conversaţii în legătură cu planificarea unor activităţi
2.5. Manifestarea interesului pentru participarea la schimbul verbal

3. Receptarea de mesaje scrise în diverse situaţii de comunicare
3.1. Extragerea informaţiilor necesare din liste sau din texte funcţionale simple (pliante, meniuri, orare, reclame)
3.2. Extragerea informațiilor din mai multe texte scurte pe baza mai multor criterii/constrângeri prestabilite sau negociate
3.3. Identificarea informaţiilor dintr-o scrisoare personală simplă/e-mail în vederea redactării unui răspuns
3.4. Manifestarea disponibilităţii pentru informare prin lectură

4. Redactarea de mesaje în diverse situaţii de comunicare
4.1. Completarea unui formular cu informaţii de identificare (educaţie, interese, competenţe)
4.2. Redactarea unei scrisori personale (inclusiv digitale) foarte simple exprimând mulțumiri sau scuze
4.3. Relatarea pe scurt a unei întâmplări utilizând cuvinte de legătură pentru a marca ordinea cronologică
4.4. Redactarea de texte simple și coerente pe teme de interes
4.5. Participarea la schimbul de mesaje scrise

6 Life choices

Vocabulary

Life events

1 ★ **Match the life events in the box to the definitions.**

get married	start school	leave home
go to university	have children	~~leave school~~
take a year out	be born	get a job
learn to drive		

1 You can do this at 16 in most of Europe, but in Germany it's 18. *leave school*
2 You need a teacher for this … and a car, of course! ________
3 The first event in life! ________
4 Lots of people do this because it helps you to get a better job. ________
5 We do this to earn money. ________
6 Some people do this so they can travel or work between school and university. ________
7 Couples do this when they want to be together forever. ________
8 Most children do this between the ages of three and six. ________
9 When this happens, you become a parent! ________
10 Everyone has to do this. You can't live with your parents forever! ________

2 ★★ **Complete the sentences with the correct form of the words from Exercise 1.**

1 Johnny Depp and Josh Hutcherson were both *born* in the state of Kentucky, USA.
2 Prince William learned to ________ when he was sixteen.
3 Salma Hayek went to ________ in Mexico City to study a degree in International Relations.
4 The actor Benedict Cumberbatch ________ a year out to teach English in Tibet.
5 Keira Knightley got ________ to her husband in the south of France.
6 Daniel Craig ________ home when he was sixteen to join the National Youth Theatre.
7 Before she was famous, Madonna got a ________ at a fast food restaurant.
8 Brad Pitt and Angelina Jolie had twins in 2008, and now they have six ________.
9 Ben Affleck and Matt Damon started the same ________ at the same time, but Affleck was in a different class.
10 The singer Katy Perry ________ school when she was 15.

3 ★★★ **Complete the second sentence so that it has the same meaning as the first. Use the life events in Exercise 1.**

1 My dad taught me to drive in his old car.
I *learned to drive in my dad's old car.*
2 I was quite happy to say goodbye to all my teachers.
I wasn't sad when I … ________
3 I'm not sure if I'm ready to look after children.
I don't know if I should … ________
4 I haven't lived in my parents' house since I was 21 years old.
I … ________
5 My first day at school was the day after my fifth birthday.
I … ________
6 My wedding was 10 years ago.
My wife and I … ________
7 I started studying Engineering when I was 18 years old.
I … ________
8 My sister's birthday is on 8 June.
My sister … ________
9 Between school and university I travelled around South America.
________ … and travelled around South America.
10 After school I started working at a computer company.
After school I … ________

4 ★★★ **What do you know about celebrities? Choose one or more and write about their life events. Write at least five sentences in your notebook.**

Taylor Swift was born in December 1989. She left school at 14 to become a singer.

Language focus 1

be going to

1 ★ **Choose the correct words in the grammar table.**

1	We use *be going to* for future **intentions / offers.**
2	They are going **have / to have** a party.
3	**We aren't / We not** going to come to your house tonight.
4	**Are you going / Are going you** to leave early?
5	Yes, **I'm going / I am.** No, he **isn't going / isn't.**

2 ★★ **Complete the sentences with *be going to* and the verbs in brackets.**

1 They *'re going to cycle* across Austria for charity. (cycle)
2 She ______________ until she's 30. (not get married)
3 He ______________ a birthday party this year. (not have)
4 We ______________ my cousins this summer. (not visit)
5 She ______________ Geography at university. (study)
6 They ______________ camping with their friends this summer. (go)
7 Theo ______________ in a bank when he leaves school. (not work)

will vs. *be going to*

3 ★★ **Circle the correct words. Use *be going to* for plans and intentions and *will* for predictions.**

Tiger x2

2022 is the Chinese year of the tiger, but the World Wildlife Fund (WWF) believes that wild tigers [1]**are going to / will** disappear completely in the next 50 years. That's why this year WWF [2]**is going to / will** start a new project called *Tiger x2*. With this project, the WWF [3]**are going to / will** try to protect 12 important areas where tigers live, and they [4]**are going to / will** use new technology to find tigers so they can stop people from killing them. Experts think this new technology [5]**is going to / will** be very important, but WWF also predicts that it [6]**isn't going to / won't** be easy. Projects like this always need a lot of money, so the news that the Leonardo DiCaprio Foundation [7]**is going to / will** help save the tigers is fantastic! They think this [8]**is going to / will** make a big difference to the tigers.

4 ★★★ **Write sentences about the plans and intentions of the people in the table.**

Danny	Sarah	Sinead
✓ climb trees in the park	✗ play tennis with Danny	✓ study for her exam
Phil	**Glen**	**Mike**
✓ invite Sinead to the cinema	✗ tidy his room	✗ call Sarah

1 *Danny's going to climb trees in the park.*
2 ______________
3 ______________
4 ______________
5 ______________
6 ______________

Explore phrasal verbs 2

5 ★★ **Complete the diary entry with the correct form of the phrasal verbs in the box.**

grow up ~~find out~~ write down go out try on get on get off

I [1] *found out* what I'm going to do tomorrow. Yesterday my mum came into my room and said: 'Tomorrow we're going to [2] ______ shopping. We're going to [3] ______ the bus and go into town. We're going to [4] ______ at Lion Road.' But why? I asked. 'We're going to buy some new school shoes for you,' she said. New shoes! I don't like shopping for shoes with my mum. We go to ten different shops and I [5] ______ one hundred different pairs. Why can't I go on my own? I asked. 'When you [6] ______, you can buy your own shoes, I promise,' she said. That's why I'm [7] ______ this ______ – so I won't forget her promise!

Listening and vocabulary

Containers and materials

1 ★ **Match the words in the box with the pictures.**

carton cardboard box glass jar can ~~plastic bag~~ paper bag crisp packet plastic bottle

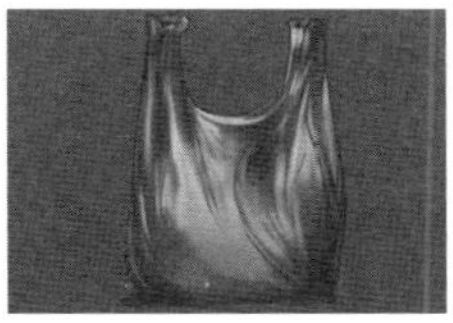

1 *plastic bag* ________

2 ________

3 ________

4 ________

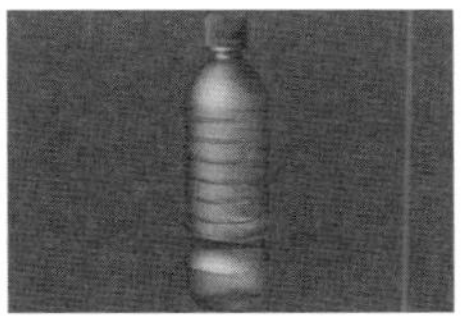

5 ________

6 ________

7 ________

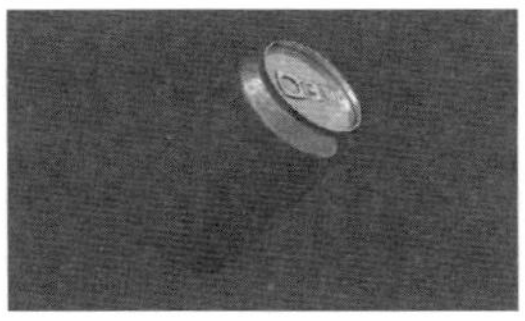

8 ________

2 ★★ **Complete the sentences with words from Exercise 1.**

1 Can I have a ___*can*___ of coke, please?
2 When I was young I made a house to play in. My 'house' was a big ________!
3 How many ________ of milk have we got?
4 Many supermarkets charge money for a ________ now, so people bring their own bags.
5 Do you need that ________? I make jam at home and I need something to put it in.
6 Some shops put your shopping in a ________ because plastic bags are bad for the environment.
7 We buy more than 50 billion ________ of water every year, but we recycle only 20% of them.

Listening

3 ★★ **Listen to Amelia talk about taking a year out. Does she think it's a good idea?**

4 ★★ **Listen again and tick the correct sentences.**

1 A gap year is usually the year before university. ✓
2 Amelia is going to take a gap year.
3 Young people can work on eco projects in their gap year.
4 Living in a different culture is easy.
5 It's a good idea to do something connected to your future studies.
6 One of Amelia's friends is going to improve her Portuguese next year.
7 A gap year can help you to improve important life skills.
8 Universities don't like students taking a gap year.

Language focus 2

Present continuous for future

1 ★ Circle the correct word in the grammar table.

We use the present continuous to talk about present / future arrangements.

2 ★★ Put the words in order to make sentences. Use contractions if possible.

1 They / the / are / housework / doing / on Sunday
They're doing the housework on Sunday.
2 am / Sonia / I / after school / seeing / not
____
3 We / meeting / tomorrow morning / at / are / eight
____
4 Two of / are / in June / leaving / my teachers
____
5 not / this school / He / staying / at / is / next year
____
6 She / driving test / taking / is / her / this afternoon
____

3 ★★ Complete the text with the present continuous form of the verbs in the box.

bring	drive	~~arrive~~	not take	not stay	take

The players 1*are arriving* at the airport at four o'clock. First, a coach 2__________ them here to the Town Hall. Then the mayor 3__________ them outside with the cup at five o'clock. They 4__________ there for a long time, because at 5:30 they 5__________ through the city to the stadium in an open-top bus. This time the players 6__________ the cup with them on the bus. They don't want any accidents.

4 ★★ Complete the conversation with the words in brackets.

A: 1*Are you going* to the basketball match tomorrow? (you / go)
B: Yes, what time 2__________? (we / meet)
A: I don't know. I 3__________ with you and Jody. My sister and I 4__________ to the dentist at 6.30. (not come; go)
A: How 5__________ to the match then? (you / get)
B: Mum 6__________ me there after the dentist. (drive)

5 ★★★ Use the information in the table to write sentences with the present continuous in the order they will happen.

Brenda	meet Freddy at 3 o'clock
Freddy	go to cinema at 7 o'clock
Johnny	drive Freddy to the cinema
Dad	come home for lunch at 2 o'clock
Me (Chloe)	leave for football practice before Dad comes home

1 *I'm leaving for football practice.*
2 ______________________
3 ______________________
4 ______________________
5 ______________________

6 ★★★ Have you made any arrangements for the weekend? For next week? What are you doing? What aren't you doing? Write at least five sentences in your notebook.

I'm not having my English class next Wednesday afternoon. I'm going to the dentist.

Explore verbs with prepositions

7 ★★ Match the sentence beginnings (1–6) with the sentence endings (a–f).

1 Tomorrow at school, we're going to learn *e*
2 How much are you going to pay ___
3 When I woke up, I was dreaming ___
4 I don't want to watch TV, so I'm going to listen ___
5 I can't go out now because I'm waiting ___
6 I don't want to spend more than £600 ___

a on a new computer.
b to some music for a while.
c for the car you're buying?
d about scoring a goal in the World Cup final!
e about the history of Poland.
f for my friend to arrive.

Reading

1 ★ **Read the text about two people and how their lives changed. What do they have in common? Circle the correct option.**

a They went from poor to rich. b They did something surprising. c They had an unhappy life.

Life choices

Mike

I was the first person in my family to go to university, and when I left I found a job in a bank in the city of London. At first I enjoyed it, and after ten years I had a good position and a great ***salary***, but I hated it! I needed a more ***rewarding*** job, so I decided to become a teacher.

I started as a volunteer in a secondary school. It was ***demanding*** but fantastic. Now I'm doing a teacher training course and next week I'm starting teaching practice. Then I'm going to look for a permanent job. Classrooms need enthusiasm and creativity. I hope I can make a difference to the young people I'll teach. People think I'm mad, but I know it's the right ***career*** choice for me!

Kirsty

She left school at 16 and learned about food at her parents' health food shop. She had her son when she was 19. He was allergic to ***dairy*** and nuts, and Kirsty couldn't find any dairy-free ice cream he could eat. So she bought a cheap ice cream machine and made her own ice cream in her kitchen. Her son loved it, her family and friends loved it, and she decided to start a business. It soon became a big success.

Now you can buy her ice cream in most UK supermarkets, and soon she's taking it to the USA. Next year she's going to ***launch*** cheap, healthy meals you can buy in the supermarket. Her business is growing, and she will be a millionaire when her son starts secondary school.

2 ★★ **Complete the definitions with the correct form of the words in bold in the text.**

1 The money that you earn in a year for your job is your *salary*.
2 Your ________ is all the different jobs that you do in your life.
3 When a company ________ a product, they sell it for the first time.
4 ________ products are foods like milk, cheese or yoghurt.
5 A ________ job is one that you like and that makes you feel good.
6 If something is ________ it is hard and needs a lot of your time and effort.

3 ★★ **Read the text in Exercise 1 again. Complete the sentences with *Mike* or *Kirsty*.**

1 *Mike* had a lot of money before.
2 ________ will be rich in the future.
3 ________ had no business experience.
4 ________ didn't like his/her career.
5 ________ went back to studying as an adult.
6 ________ has made a decision people don't understand.
7 ________ created something new.

4 ★★★ **Whose story was more surprising, Mike's or Kirsty's? Why? Do you know anyone who had a big change in their life? What did they do?**

Writing

A thank you email

1 Read Hayley's email to her aunt. How did she help Hayley?

Dear Auntie Jane,

I'm writing to thank you for helping me choose Mum's 50th birthday present.

I had no idea what to get her so I really enjoyed looking for a present with you. She loved the earrings we chose.

Dad gave her a holiday to Venice. They're planning to go for two weeks and while they're away, I'm going to stay with Nicole, my best friend. I'll need to sleep on her sofa, but I don't mind doing that. It'll be fun!

Anyway, I should go now because I promised to help with the dinner tonight and I have to finish doing my homework.

Thanks again for all your help.

Hayley

2 Read the email again. Answer the questions.

1 How old is Hayley's mum? ____________
2 What did Hayley buy for her mum? ____________
3 Where is her mum going with her dad? ____________
4 Who is Nicole? ____________
5 Where is Hayley going when her parents are on holiday? ____________

Useful language Verb patterns

3 Look back at Hayley's email. Complete the phrases with the words in the text.

1 I really enjoyed *looking for a present with you*.
2 They're planning ____________.
3 I'll need ____________.
4 I don't mind ____________.
5 I promised ____________.
6 I have to finish ____________.

4 Complete the sentences with the correct form of the verbs in the box below.

help	study	watch	play	buy	~~take~~

1 My teacher is planning *to take* our class on a school trip.
2 My brother enjoys ____________ computer games with his friends.
3 I have an exam tomorrow so I need ____________ tonight.
4 We finished ____________ the film at 8 p.m. last night.
5 They promised ____________ me a tablet for my birthday.
6 I don't mind ____________ you with your homework.

Writing

UNIT 6

5 Complete the sentences with the correct question words.

where how many how ~~what~~ when

1 It's my friend's party and I don't know *what* to wear.
2 My mum and dad are trying to decide ________ to go on holiday.
3 Let's talk about ________ to have the party – how about next Friday?
4 I'm writing to ask you ________ to make a very important decision in my life.
5 I'm not sure ________ people to invite to the party. I think 20 friends will be enough.

6 Circle the correct option.

1 I'd like to thank you **of** / **for** all your help.
2 I want to talk **to** / **with** you about something.
3 My dad's thinking **to** / **of** taking my mum on a romantic weekend.
4 Did you hear **of** / **about** the present I got from Uncle Hugh?
5 I'm writing **to** / **for** you to say thanks.

WRITING TIP

Make it better! ✓✓✓
Include different phrases to say thank you.
Thank you so much.
It's very kind of you.

7 Which of these is not a phrase to say thank you?

1 Thanks a lot!
2 I really appreciate it.
3 I'm writing to thank you for the beautiful present.
4 Did you say thanks to your mum?
5 Thank you so much for everything.

8 Look back at Hayley's email. Tick (✓) the information she includes.

1 the reason for writing ☐
2 what happened ☐
3 other news ☐
4 her aunt's health ☐
5 future plans ☐
6 phrases to say thank you ☐

PLAN

9 You are going to write a thank you email to a friend or family member who helped you. Choose one of the situations below. Then use the ideas in Exercise 8 and make notes.

________ helped me with …

1 a present
2 a holiday
3 a decision
4 organising a party

WRITE

10 Write the thank you email. Look at page 79 of the Student's Book to help you.

____
____
____
____
____
____
____
____
____
____
____
____

CHECK

11 Check your writing. Can you say YES to these questions?

- Did you use the ideas in Exercise 8?
- Do you use the correct verb patterns?
- Do you use prepositions correctly?
- Do you use different phrases to say thank you?

Do you need to write a second draft?

6 Review

Vocabulary

Life events

1 Match the sentence halves.

1 I want to travel around the world when I _*c*_
2 I want to study Art when I go to ___
3 I was 25 when my first child was ___
4 I was 18 when I ___
5 I want to buy a car, but first, I need to learn ___
6 After I leave university, I want to ___
7 If I meet the right person, I'll probably get ___

a to drive.
b left school.
c take a year out.
d university.
e get a job.
f married.
g born.

☐ Total: 6

Containers and materials

2 Write the words in the box under the correct picture. You can use some words more than once.

bag	bottle	box	can	cardboard	carton
crisp packet	~~glass jar~~	paper	plastic		

1 _*glass*_ _*jar*_

2 ________ ________

3 ________ ________

4 ________ ________

5 ________

6 ________

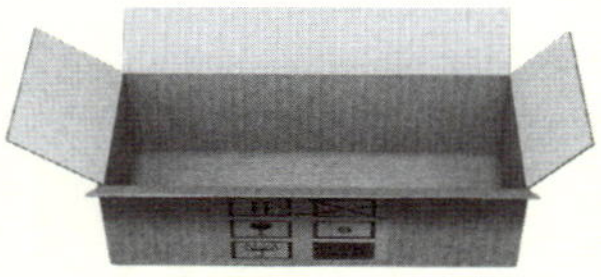

7 ________ ________

8 ________ ________

☐ Total: 7

Language focus

be going to

3 Complete the conversation with the correct form of *be going to* and the verbs in brackets.

Jack: What [1] _*are you going to do*_ (you / do) this summer?
Rosie: I [2] ________________ (work) on a farm. How about you? [3] ________________ (you / do) anything special?
Jack: Well, I [4] ________________ (not work)!
Rosie: [5] ________________ (you / travel)?
Jack: Yes, I am. My brother [6] ________________ (sail) to Alaska and he [7] ________________ (take) me with him!
Rosie: That sounds amazing!

☐ Total: 6

will vs. *be going to*

4 Complete the sentences with *be going to* for future plans and intentions, or *will* for predictions. Use the verbs in brackets.

1 I think more people _*will recycle*_ in the future. (recycle)
2 I ____________ all my homework on Friday night before I go out. (do)
3 He's a very good footballer – I think he ____________ for Brazil one day! (play)
4 We ____________ petrol in cars in the future. (not use)
5 Danny and Sara ____________ house in six months. (move)
6 We ____________ the football tonight, we've got other plans. (not watch)

☐ Total: 5

Present continuous for future

5 Write sentences with the present continuous about Jeannine's plans.

1 *She's playing basketball at 5 o'clock on Monday.*
2 ______
3 ______
4 ______
5 ______
6 ______

Monday	play basketball at 5 o'clock
Tuesday	do Maths exam at 3 o'clock
Wednesday	go to Tom's party at 7 o'clock
Thursday	go to the cinema with Katrina at 8 o'clock
Friday	go swimming after school
Saturday	do yoga in the afternoon

Total: 5

Language builder

6 Circle the correct options.

Jake: I [1]______ Japan on a student exchange.
Naomi: Really? I [2]______ to Japan last year. I had [3]______ time!
Jake: Can you give me [4]______ advice? What [5]______ I take with me?
Naomi: Take a really good camera. I took [6]______ fantastic photos on my trip. [7]______ any Japanese?
Jake: I study Japanese at school. That's why I [8]______ on this trip. But I'm not as good as some of the others in my class.

1 (a) am going to visit b will visit c visit
2 a go b going c went
3 a best b the best c the better
4 a much b any c many
5 a should b must c will
6 a some b any c much
7 a Are you speaking b You speaking c Do you speak
8 a go b am going c will go

Total: 7

Vocabulary builder

7 Circle the correct options.

1 We buy milk in ______ or glass bottles.
(a) cartons b paper bags c glass jars
2 After lunch, my dad washed all the plates in the ______.
a mirror b sink c desk
3 Does your ______ make photocopies?
a printer b memory stick c tablet
4 For me, ______ is being with my friends.
a illness b kindness c happiness
5 I enjoyed my job and I used to ______ a lot of money.
a sell b earn c shop
6 I'd like to ______ children in the future.
a make b do c have
7 I spend a lot of money ______ clothes.
a to b on c for
8 Can you help me ______ the washing, please?
a do b make c have
9 Before I go to university, I'll ______ a year out.
a go b be c take
10 When I ______, I want to be a photographer.
a grow up b am born c get on
11 As soon as I'm eighteen, I'm going to ______ home.
a go b leave c buy

Total: 10

Speaking

8 Put the conversation in the correct order.

1 ___ B: Absolutely. That's a much better idea.
2 ___ A: Do you think university students should get a weekend job?
3 ___ A: I suppose you're right. Do you think they should get a job in the holidays?
4 ___ B: Maybe, but I also think they need that time to study.

Total: 4

Writing

9 Write a thank you email to your friend, Mike. Thank him for helping you study for an important exam which you passed. Invite him to go to the cinema with you. Write 25–35 words.

Total: 10

Total: 60

Get it right! Unit 6

will vs. *be going to*

Remember that:

- we use ***be going to*** to talk about future plans and intentions.
  ✓ ***I'm going to*** *study on Saturday night.*
  ✗ ~~*I will study on Saturday night.*~~
- we use ***will***, not *be going to*, to talk about predictions.
  ✓ *If I can, I* ***will*** *call you tomorrow.*
  ✗ ~~*If I can, I'm going to call you tomorrow.*~~

1 Circle the correct words.

New mail

Hi Zara,
I'm glad you [1] **will / are going to** come to the festival with us next weekend. Here are the plans – [2] **we'll / we're going** to meet at the train station at 11:30 and [3] **we're going to / we'll** get a train at midday. There [4] **are going to / will** be lots of bands on in the afternoon and they probably [5] **aren't going to / won't** finish until around midnight. Do you think your dad [6] **will / is going to** pick us up if we ask him?
Thanks,
Lily

Present continuous for future

Remember that:

- we use the present continuous to talk about future plans and intentions.
  ✓ *He****'s going*** *to Brazil on holiday this summer.*
- we use the present simple to talk about facts, habits and routines.
  ✓ *She* ***visits*** *her grandparents every summer.*

2 Are the sentences correct? Correct the incorrect sentences.

1 At the weekend he is sleeping until 9 o'clock in the morning.
At the weekend, he sleeps until 9 o'clock in the morning.
2 They are flying to Moscow next Wednesday.
______
3 John plays the piano in the school concert this year.
______
4 My friends have a party next Saturday.
______
5 He always travels to school by bus.
______

Verbs with prepositions

Remember, some verbs take a preposition between the verb and the indirect object. Don't forget the preposition!

✓ *I enjoy* ***listening to*** *my MP3 player on the bus.*
✗ ~~*I enjoy listening my MP3 player on the bus.*~~

3 Are the sentences correct? Add the correct preposition where necessary.

1 I will wait *for* you in front of the cinema.
2 They listened the radio this morning.
3 If you haven't got any money, I will pay the tickets.
4 Young people often dream flying.
5 Do you spend a lot of money books?
6 I want to learn English on the internet.

Time expressions

Remember that:

- we use ***on*** before dates and days of the week.
  ✓ *I flew to Paris* ***on*** *6 July.*
- we use ***in*** before months, seasons and years.
  ✓ *I went to Paris* ***in*** *July.*
- we use ***at*** before the time.
  ✓ *The plane landed* ***at*** *6:45 p.m.*
- we don't usually use a preposition before ***next/last/this week/month/morning***, etc.
  ✓ *I am going to Argentina* ***next summer***.
  ✗ ~~*I am going to Argentina on next summer.*~~

4 Correct five more mistakes in the dialogue.

Rory: Hi, Karen, what are you doing?
Karen: I'm going to the dentist ~~on~~ *at* 10 o'clock. Then, on this afternoon, I'm meeting Sarah to talk about our holiday. We're going to Italy with her parents on July!
Rory: Wow! That's exciting. What are you doing this evening?
Karen: I'm going to the cinema. The film begins on 8 o'clock. Do you want to come with us?
Rory: Oh, thank you, but I can't. I've got an exam at next week, so I have to study. The exam's on Tuesday. Maybe we can go to the cinema on next Saturday? I think there's usually a film at about 2 o'clock.
Karen: Great! See you there! Good luck with your exam.

7 Look out!

General and specific competences from the curriculum explored in the unit

1. Understand oral messages in different communication situations
1.1. Identify essential information from the news presented on TV/recorded materials related to different events, when the comment is illustrated by pictures
1.2. Identify details from messages and interactions on predictable topics, when the speakers/interlocutors talk clearly and slowly
1.3. Identify specific aspects of the culture of the language studied

2. Speak in different communication situations
2.1. Present plans, intentions and future projects
2.2. Give a short and simple presentation on activities
2.3. Initiate, continue and finish a dialogue on familiar or personal interest topics
2.4. Participate in conversations related to planning activities
2.5. Show interest in participating in a verbal exchange

3. Understand written messages in different communication situations
3.1. Select necessary information from lists or simple functional texts (brochures, menus, schedules, ads)
3.2. Extract information from multiple short texts based on several predefined or negotiated criteria/constraints
3.3. Identify information from a simple written letter/email to write an answer
3.4. Show willingness to be informed through reading

4. Write messages in everyday communication situations
4.1. Complete a form with personally identifiable information (education, interests, competences)
4.2. Write a very simple personal letter (digital version included) to express thanks or apologies
4.3. Tell a story, in short, using linkers to emphasise the chronological order
4.4. Write simple and coherent texts on specific topics of interest
4.5. Participate in the exchange of written messages

Competenţele generale şi specifice din programa şcolară, urmărite în unitatea de învăţare

1. Receptarea de mesaje orale în diverse situaţii de comunicare
1.1. Identificarea informaţiilor esenţiale din ştirile prezentate la TV/materiale înregistrate, referitoare la diferite evenimente, atunci când comentariul este ilustrat prin imagini
1.2. Identificarea detaliilor din mesaje şi interacţiuni pe subiecte previzibile când locutorii/interlocutorii vorbesc clar şi rar
1.3. Identificarea unor elemente culturale specifice limbii studiate

2. Exprimarea orală în diverse situaţii de comunicare
2.1. Prezentarea unor planuri/unor intenţii şi proiecte de viitor
2.2. Descrierea scurtă, elementară a unor activităţi
2.3. Iniţierea, susţinerea şi încheierea unui dialog pe teme familiare sau de interes personal
2.4. Participarea la conversaţii în legătură cu planificarea unor activităţi
2.5. Manifestarea interesului pentru participarea la schimbul verbal

3. Receptarea de mesaje scrise în diverse situaţii de comunicare
3.1. Extragerea informaţiilor necesare din liste sau din texte funcţionale simple (pliante, meniuri, orare, reclame)
3.2. Extragerea informaţiilor din mai multe texte scurte pe baza mai multor criterii/constrângeri prestabilite sau negociate
3.3. Identificarea informaţiilor dintr-o scrisoare personală simplă/e-mail în vederea redactării unui răspuns
3.4. Manifestarea disponibilităţii pentru informare prin lectură

4. Redactarea de mesaje în diverse situaţii de comunicare
4.1. Completarea unui formular cu informaţii de identificare (educaţie, interese, competenţe)
4.2. Redactarea unei scrisori personale (inclusiv digitale) foarte simple exprimând mulţumiri sau scuze
4.3. Relatarea pe scurt a unei întâmplări utilizând cuvinte de legătură pentru a marca ordinea cronologică
4.4. Redactarea de texte simple şi coerente pe teme de interes
4.5. Participarea la schimbul de mesaje scrise

7 Look out!

Vocabulary

Accidents and injuries

1 ★ Find nine more verbs for accidents and injuries in the word search. Write them under the pictures.

c	r	a	s	h	h	f	o	l	b
p	l	e	h	i	n	u	n	e	r
s	f	a	l	l	g	t	r	g	e
m	l	d	a	n	b	r	r	t	a
t	e	i	l	o	u	a	c	o	k
r	a	x	p	p	r	p	b	u	t
i	n	d	l	r	n	n	r	i	t
p	r	e	b	a	n	g	v	b	e

1 *hurt* your back

2 ________ over the dog

3 ________ your car

4 ________ your finger

5 ________ your head

6 ________ off your bike

7 ________ on ice

8 ________ your leg

9 ________ your hand

10 ________ your fingers

2 ★★ Complete the sentences with the past tense of the verbs from Exercise 1.

1 When I was ten I *fell off* my bike and __________ my leg. I couldn't do sport for ages!
2 The man was really tall so he __________ his head when he went through the door.
3 The robber __________ over a dog and dropped the woman's bag.
4 Someone __________ their car outside our school yesterday. Everyone heard the noise.
5 He wanted to cook a fried egg and he __________ his hand on the hot cooker.
6 On his way to the shops, my granddad __________ on some ice and __________ his back.
7 She __________ her finger when she tried to open a can.

3 ★★ Circle the wrong word.

1 I banged my (car) / head / knee.
2 She fell off / broke / hurt her skateboard.
3 He broke / hurt / tripped his leg skiing.
4 You trapped your foot / finger / chest.
5 I cut / fell / burnt my finger yesterday.
6 He tripped over the dog / your bike / the house.

4 ★★★ Complete the story with the correct form of the words in the box.

trip/over	fall off/bike	burn/hand
cut/finger	~~hurt/back~~	crash/car
bang/head		

Yesterday there were a lot of accidents in our house. My dad [1]*hurt his back* when he tried to move the sofa. My mum [2]__________ when she opened a can of cat food and then later she [3]__________ when she cooked the dinner. Then my granddad [4]__________ the cat and [5]__________ on the wall. My sister went cycling in the park and [6]__________ . She couldn't walk and her leg hurt, so we all went to the hospital in Dad's car. Then Dad [7]__________ into an ambulance! I was fine!

5 ★★★ Do you know anyone who has a lot of accidents? Have your friends had an accident or injured themselves? Write at least five sentences in your notebook.

When Jamie was six, he fell off a wall and broke his arm.

Language focus 1

Present perfect

1 ★ **Complete the rules in the grammar table with the words in the box.**

hasn't has when have haven't

1	We use the present perfect to talk about things in the past. We don't know exactly ________ they happened.
2	Affirmative: I/We/You/They ________ + past participle He/She/It ________ + past participle
3	Negative: I/We/You/They ________ + past participle He/She/It ________ + past participle

2 ★★ **Write the past participle of the verbs in the table.**

crash	ride
1 *crashed*	2 ________
fall	teach
3 ________	4 ________
meet	break
5 ________	6 ________
slip	go
7 ________	8 ________

3 ★★ **Complete the sentences with the present perfect form of the verbs from Exercise 2.**

1 Jackie *hasn't met* a famous person. (✗)
2 I ________ my arm twice in the same place! (✓)
3 They ________ to hospital ten times! (✓)
4 We ________ a motorbike, but we want to! (✗)
5 Fred ________ his car, but he's OK. (✓)
6 She ________ on some ice in the street. (✓)
7 You ________ off your bike today. You're getting better! (✗)
8 My English teacher ________ at this school for very long. (✗)

4 ★★ **Complete the text with the present perfect form of the verbs in brackets.**

My friends and I did an internet quiz called *50 things to do before you're 18*. All of us [1] *have been* (be) camping, but we [2] ________ (not have) a holiday without adults. We [3] ________ (watch) a film in 3D. We [4] ________ (not meet) a famous person, but I [5] ________ (see) Penelope Cruz in the street. David [6] ________ (hold) a snake at a safari park, and Alicia [7] ________ (sing) in a concert – actually, lots of concerts! We [8] ________ (not do) anything dangerous like bungee jumping. But we're only 15 so there's lots of time!

5 ★★★ **Write sentences about what Candice has and hasn't done.**

crash her bike	do something dangerous	break her leg	meet someone famous	ride a horse
✓	✓	✗	✗	✓

1 *She has crashed her bike.*
2 ________
3 ________
4 ________
5 ________

Explore expressions with *get*

6 ★★ **Match the sentence beginnings (1–6) with the sentence endings (a–f).**

1 Yesterday I missed the bus and got *e*
2 I'm sorry you're not feeling well and I hope you get ___
3 I've never slipped on ice and got ___
4 If I go home late, my mum gets ___
5 I hate sitting in the back of the car because I always get ___
6 Do you know anyone who doesn't want to get ___

a injured.
b married?
c better soon.
d sick.
e home late.
f worried.

Listening and vocabulary

The body

1 ★★ **Use the picture to complete the crossword.**

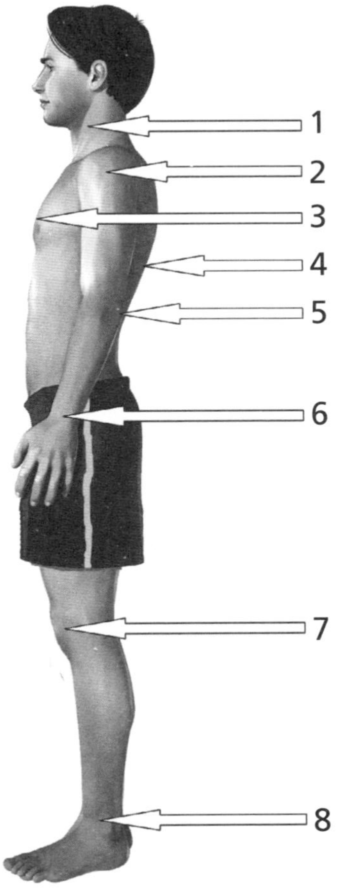

2 ★★★ **Write the correct parts of the body from Exercise 1.**

1 You shouldn't put these on the table while you're eating. *elbows*
2 This is always behind you. ________
3 You cannot break this. ________
4 This is where you put your watch. ________
5 You use this to move your head. ________
6 Hang your schoolbag from these. ________
7 When you fall over you usually hurt these. ________
8 Your socks help to keep these warm. ________

Listening

3 ★★ **Listen to Sophie talking to her friend Rob about extreme sports. Tick (✓) the sports that Sophie has done.**

canyoning

parkour

bungee jumping

hang-gliding

canyoning	✓	climbing	☐
football	☐	hang-gliding	☐
kitesurfing	☐	parkour	☐
rafting	☐	running	☐
snowboarding	☐	tennis	☐
volleyball	☐	windsurfing	☐

4 ★★ **Listen again and choose the correct options.**

1 What does Sophie say about canyoning?
   (a) It's dangerous.
   b She's tried it once.
   c She's had an accident.
2 Sophie explains that …
   a she likes being scared.
   b she never gets frightened.
   c she doesn't take risks.
3 Rob says that he …
   a hasn't done any sport.
   b likes being scared too.
   c enjoys safer sports.
4 Sophie hasn't been bungee jumping because …
   a her parents think it's too expensive.
   b she isn't old enough.
   c she prefers other sports.
5 Sophie explains that parkour …
   a is only practised in France.
   b isn't very difficult.
   c is a sport you do in a city.
6 What is true about Sophie?
   a She's fallen off her bike.
   b She's broken her shoulder.
   c She's crashed her surfboard.

Language focus 2

Present perfect: questions

1 ★ **Circle the correct words in the grammar table.**

1	We use questions in the present perfect to ask about **present / past** experiences.
2	**Have / Has** you ever **be / been** to Spain? **Have / Has** your brother **started / start** university?
3	To ask about your **whole life / recent experiences** put *ever* **before / after** the subject.
4	Have they **ever tried / tried ever** bungee jumping? Yes, they **has / have**.

2 ★★ **Write questions with the present perfect. Then match the questions to the answers.**

1 Jack / go / kitesurfing?
Has Jack been kitesurfing? ___ *b*

2 it / snow / a lot?
______________ ___

3 your parents / crash / their car / ever / ?
______________ ___

4 Helen / cut / her hand?
______________ ___

5 we / see / this film about a plane crash / ever / ?
______________ ___

6 you / break / your arm / ever / ?
______________ ___

a Yes, I have. Twice!
b No, he hasn't.
c No, they haven't.
d Yes, we have. Last month!
e Yes, she has. In Art class.
f Yes, it has. Look out for ice!

3 ★★★ **Write questions in the present perfect for these answers.**

1 *Have you ever broken a part of your body?*
Yes, I have. I broke my leg last year.

2 ______________
No, I haven't, but I'd like to visit Rio.

3 ______________
Yes, I have. I went to see Beyoncé last October.

4 ______________
I'm not sure. I think I've read about 30 books in my life.

5 ______________
Yes, I have. I fell off my bike once and hurt my leg.

6 ______________
Yes, we have. We had a cat a few years ago.

Past simple vs. present perfect

4 ★★ **Complete the sentences with the correct form of the past simple or present perfect and the verbs in brackets.**

1 I *fell off* my bike yesterday and hurt my arm. (fall off)
2 My brother ______ his leg three times. He loves dangerous sports. (break)
3 I've eaten rabbit, but I ______ horse. (eat)
4 My sister ______ married in 2010. (get)
5 I ______ snowboarding with my family in December. (go)
6 My best friend ______ a new tablet. It's amazing! (buy)
7 I ______ at 7 a.m. this morning. (get up)
8 They ______ to New York, but we haven't. (go)

Explore compound nouns

5 ★ **Match the parts of the compound words.**

1 forest — *b*
2 charity
3 fire
4 fishing
5 wild

a life
b floor
c worker
d wood
e boat

6 ★★ **Complete the sentences with the words in Exercise 5.**

1 I've always wanted to be a *charity worker* to help people in need.
2 My uncle has a ______ and we sometimes go on the lake in it.
3 We'll need lots of ______ to keep warm when we go camping.
4 I love watching TV programmes about ______ – especially about African animals.
5 In the morning, we saw some rabbits running across the ______.

Reading

1 ★ **Read the text about a town in Canada. What is Churchill trying to do about polar bears?**

POLAR BEAR ALERT

Churchill, on Hudson Bay in Manitoba, Northern Canada, is the polar bear capital of the world. The town has over 800 ***inhabitants*** and close by there are about the same number of bears!

The town of Churchill and the bears lived together peacefully for 300 years with only two fatal bear attacks. However, climate change has made ***co-existence*** more difficult. The ice ***season*** in Hudson Bay has got shorter, and this has made it difficult for them to find food in spring and autumn. So, many bears are ***starving*** and coming to look for food in Churchill. Despite the changes in Churchill, one thing stays the same: when the Hudson Bay freezes over in the winter, the bears leave town to hunt seals on the ice.

Churchill wants bears and humans to co-exist, so it has a Polar Bear ***Alert*** programme, managed by Manitoba Conservation. The idea is not to kill the bears, but to make them scared of people so they run away. The Conservation staff has different ways to scare the bears: a pistol with blanks, a noisy air horn, firecrackers, even a paintball gun! There is also a special bear 'jail' if they don't run away. Then, Manitoba Conservation takes these bears back into the tundra by helicopter.

Members of the Conservation patrol Churchill 24-hours a day. In November, one of the most dangerous months, there are often 20 alerts a day. Luckily, most ***encounters*** between people and bears in Churchill haven't been serious. One woman threw a bag of shopping at a bear to scare it away. Most of the bears are sub-adult males. 'Teenagers,' said one officer. 'They're the ones that get into trouble.'

2 ★★ **Match the words in bold in the text with the definitions.**

1 Summer, winter, spring or autumn. *season*
2 When different people or things live together. ______
3 A warning to tell people something dangerous could happen. ______
4 When a person or animal is very hungry because there is no food to eat. ______
5 The people who live in a place. ______
6 When people or animals meet by chance. ______

3 ★★ **Read the text again and answer the questions.**

1 How many polar bears live near Churchill?
About 800.
2 What is the effect of climate change on the people and bears?
______
3 Have they attacked anyone in the town recently?
______
4 What does the Polar Bear Alert programme try to do?
______
5 What does the Conservation staff use to frighten the bears?
______
6 What do they do with bears that don't leave the town?
______

4 **Write three or four questions to ask Manitoba Conservation or one of the people who saw a bear in the town. Then write the answers – you can invent them!**

______
______
______
______
______
______
______
______
______
______

Writing

An email refusing an invitation

1 Read Edward's email. Why can't he go camping?

YourMAIL | New | Reply | Delete | Junk

Hi George,

Thanks for writing to me about the camping trip next weekend. I'm sorry, I'd love to go with you and your classmates, but I can't. My cousin's getting married that weekend. I didn't tell you before because I completely forgot about it. My mum told me months ago and I put it in my phone, but then I lost the phone!

He's going to have the party on the beach. I've never been to a beach party before so it'll be fun. All my cousins are going to be there. I haven't seen them since last summer. So how about another weekend?

Sorry again! If you can't change the dates, have a great time. I'll send you some photos of the party.

Enjoy yourselves!

Edward

2 Read Edward's email again. Answer the questions.

1 When did Edward's mum tell him about the party? ______
2 Why did Edward forget about it? ______
3 Where is the party going to be? ______
4 When did Edward last see his cousins? ______
5 What will he send George? ______

Useful language Polite language for refusing

3 Find expressions in Edward's email with the same meaning as the sentences below.

1 Sorry, I can't come.
I'm sorry, I'd love to go with you, but I can't.
2 Have fun.
______
3 I'm really sorry.
______
4 Could we go another weekend?
______

4 Put the words in order to make sentences that explain why you need to refuse an invitation.

1 hurt / leg / fell / I / and / my
I fell and hurt my leg.
2 party / are / My / having / a / cousins
______
3 Monday / I / an / have to / on / study / exam / for
______
4 bike / arm / fell off / my / my / I / broke / and
______
5 70th / and / surprise party / birthday / we're / my / having / It's / a / grandmother's
______

5 Some verbs in English have two objects. Rewrite the sentences so the direct object in the first sentence comes at the end of the new sentence.

1 My parents bought a present for me.
My parents bought me a present.
2 Helen showed the photos of the party to me.
______
3 We gave a surprise to my dad.
______
4 Jeff sent the video to me.
______
5 Aidan lent his bike to me for the weekend.
______
6 My mum found some tickets for me.
______

Writing

WRITING TIP

Make it better! ✓✓✓
Finish the email by telling your friends to have a good time.
I hope you have a great time at the concert.

6 Which sentence does <u>not</u> tell someone to have a good time?

1 Enjoy yourselves!
2 I'm sorry I'm going to miss it.
3 I hope you have a great time.
4 I hope you like the camp.
5 Have a great weekend!

7 Write the information in the order it is in Edward's email.

apologise again
say why you can't go to the event
close the email
suggest another time to meet
~~apologise~~

1 *apologise*
2 ________
3 ________
4 ________
5 ________

PLAN

8 You are going to write an email refusing an invitation to a friend or family member. Use the ideas below to help you. Then make notes.

You've been invited to …

a family party   a concert   the cinema   a party

You can't go because …

you/your friend had an accident
you haven't got enough money
you are busy that day

WRITE

9 Write the email. Look at page 93 of the Student's Book to help you.

CHECK

10 Check your writing. Can you say YES to these questions?

- Did you use the ideas in Exercise 8?
- Did you use polite language for refusing the invitation?
- Did you explain why you can't go?
- Did you use verbs with two objects correctly?
- Did you tell your friends to have a good time?
- Did you write the information in your email in the correct order?

Do you need to write a second draft?

7 Review

Vocabulary

Accidents and injuries

1 Match the sentence halves.

1 I hurt *b*
2 I burnt ___
3 I cut ___
4 I slipped ___
5 I broke ___
6 I banged ___
7 I tripped ___

a my finger on that big knife.
b my back trying to lift some boxes.
c my hand when I touched a hot plate.
d my head on the table.
e my leg when I fell off my bike.
f over the dog when I ran into the kitchen.
g on the ice when I went skating.

Total: 6

The body

2 Write the name for each part of the body.

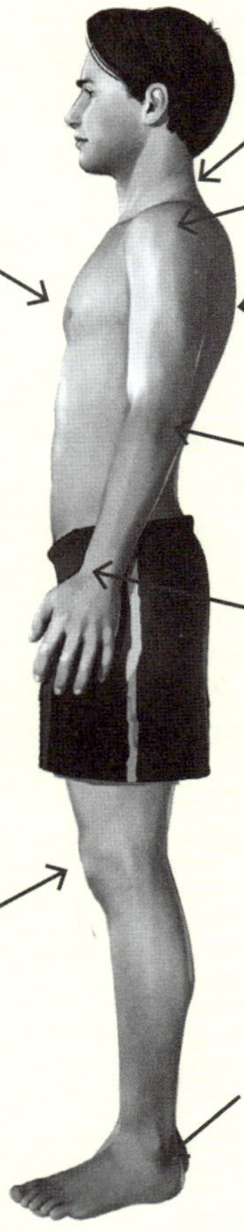

1 n *eck* ________
2 c ________
3 s ________
4 b ________
5 e ________
6 w ________
7 k ________
8 a ________

Total: 7

Language focus

Present perfect: affirmative and negative

3 Complete the email with the present perfect form of the verbs in brackets.

Hi Julie,

We're having fun on holiday. My parents love climbing, but we [1] *haven't climbed* (not climb) any hills because mum [2] ________ (hurt) her ankle and can't walk very well!
We [3] ________ (go) to the beach, and I [4] ________ (have) some surfing lessons.
My sister [5] ________ (try) ten different flavours of ice cream. How about you? How was your holiday?

Tania

Total: 4

Present perfect: questions

4 Put the words in order to make questions. Use the past participle form of the verbs in brackets.

1 ever / you / (write) / a diary / Have
Have you ever written a diary ?
2 ever / your brother / Has / a competition / (win)
________ ?
3 (eat) / ever / you / shark / Have
________ ?
4 you / Have / (break) / ever / your ankle
________ ?
5 Have / your parents / (visit) / Australia / ever
________ ?
6 your sister / in a concert / (play) / Has / violin / ever
________ ?

Total: 5

Past simple vs. present perfect

5 Circle the correct options.

1 Barak Obama **has become** / **became** the US president in 2009.
2 **Has your country ever had** / **Did your country ever have** a woman president?
3 Astronauts Neil Armstrong and Buzz Aldrin **have walked** / **walked** on the moon in July 1969.
4 The Wright brothers **have invented** / **invented** the world's first aeroplane.
5 Around 40% of Americans **travelled** / **have travelled** to another country.

Total: 4

Language builder

6 Circle the correct options to complete the conversation.

Liz: Have you ever [1] ___________ any bones?
Jamie: Yes, I [2] ___________ my arm when I [3] ___________ skiing in Italy last winter.
Liz: That's terrible! [4] ___________ it really painful?
Jamie: Yes! I [5] ___________ use my arm for about three months.
Liz: I [6] ___________ skiing this winter. I hope I don't have an accident! What [7] ___________ I wear?
Jamie: You [8] ___________ wear a helmet. That's very important, and you [9] ___________ ski on your own.
Liz: That's good advice. Do you think snowboarding is [10] ___________ than skiing?
Jamie: Skiing is [11] ___________ than snowboarding because you can turn more quickly.

1 a break b broke (c) broken
2 a break b broke c broken
3 a was b have c were
4 a Did b Was c Were
5 a couldn't b shouldn't c haven't
6 a will go b am going to go c go
7 a will b should c could
8 a should b could c must
9 a mustn't b couldn't c won't
10 a most dangerous b more dangerous c dangerous
11 a less dangerous b the least dangerous c dangerous

Total: 10

Vocabulary builder

7 Circle the correct options.

1 Have you ever ___________ your car?
a hurt b slipped (c) crashed
2 Tom fell off his bike and ___________ injured.
a did b got c turned
3 You haven't written ___________ the new words.
a on b down c for
4 Why did you ___________ your towel at me?
a catch b jump c throw
5 I can't hear you. ___________ the music!
a Turn down b Turn up c Shut down
6 My mum ___________ on ice and hurt her ankle.
a banged b tripped c slipped
7 We haven't put the books in cardboard ___________.
a packets b bags c boxes
8 My brother was sick last week, but he's getting ___________.
a better b good c home
9 She was very ___________ because she didn't cry when she broke her wrist.
a funny b brave c kind
10 Go ___________ or you'll fall off your bike.
a well b quietly c slowly

Total: 9

Speaking

8 Complete the conversations with words from the box.

terrible	no	~~up~~	shame	sorry	How

1 A: Hi, Caroline!
B: Hi Sam, what have you been ___up___ to?
2 A: I hurt my finger.
B: What a ___________!
3 A: I've burned my wrist.
B: That's ___________!
4 A: Someone stole my bicycle!
B: I'm ___________ to hear that.
5 A: I've passed all my exams!
B: ___________ amazing!
6 A: I've hurt my hand.
B: Oh ___________!

Total: 5

Total: 50

Get it right! Unit 7

Present perfect

Remember that:

- we use subject + ***have*** + past participle to talk about past experiences. Don't forget to use ***have***!
  ✓ *He can't play football because he **has** broken his leg.*
  ✗ ~~*He can't play football because he broken his leg.*~~
- we use ***have*** + subject + past participle to ask questions about past experiences.
  ✓ ***Has** he broken his leg?*
  ✗ ~~*He has broken his leg?*~~

1 Find and correct seven more mistakes in the email.

New mail

Hi Tim,
I can't come to the picnic this afternoon! My dad can't drive me to the park because he ^*has* hurt his back. My brother can't bring me because he injured his foot. My sister fell off her bike and she thinks she broken her arm. And I have to stay at home because my dog eaten something bad. As for Martin, I not heard from him. You have seen him this week? I hope he not had an accident too!

ever or *never*?

Remember that:

- we can use ***ever*** or ***never*** to talk about experiences in the past.
- we use *have* + subject + ***ever*** + past participle to make questions.
  ✓ *Have you **ever** eaten fried insects?*
  ✗ ~~*You have ever eaten fried insects?*~~
- we use ***ever***, not ***never***, in statements after superlative adjectives.
  ✓ *It's the most serious accident he has **ever** had.*
  ✗ ~~*It's the most serious accident he has never had.*~~
- we do not use ***never*** in sentences that are already negative.
  ✓ *They have **never** been to Asia.*
  ✓ *They haven't **ever** been to Asia.*
  ✗ ~~*They haven't never been to Asia.*~~

2 Are the sentences correct? Correct the incorrect sentences.

1 I never have been to Australia.
I have never been to Australia.
2 It was the best party I have never been to.
______
3 You have ever travelled on an aeroplane?
______
4 This smartphone is the best phone I have ever had.
______
5 He's had a lot of accidents, but he hasn't never broken any bones.
______
6 He told us he has ever spoken English outside class.
______
7 Have they never been in hospital?
______

Spell it right! Past participles

Remember that:

- with irregular verbs, the past simple form of the verb and the past participle are often different. Look at the irregular verb table on page 127 of the Student's Book.
  ✓ *John **fell** (past simple) off his bike last week.*
  ✓ *Come quickly! John **has fallen** (past participle) off his bike.*

3 Write the correct past simple and past participle form of the verbs.

Infinitive	Past simple	Past participle
eat	*ate*	*eaten*
see	______	______
swim	______	______
fly	______	______
sing	______	______
write	______	______
speak	______	______
break	______	______
fall	______	______
have	______	______
take	______	______

8 Having fun

General and specific competences from the curriculum explored in the unit

1. Understand oral messages in different communication situations
1.1. Identify essential information from the news presented on TV/recorded materials related to different events, when the comment is illustrated by pictures
1.2. Identify details from messages and interactions on predictable topics, when the speakers/interlocutors talk clearly and slowly
1.3. Identify specific aspects of the culture of the language studied

2. Speak in different communication situations
2.1. Present plans, intentions and future projects
2.2. Give a short and simple presentation on activities
2.3. Initiate, continue and finish a dialogue on familiar or personal interest topics
2.4. Participate in conversations related to planning activities
2.5. Show interest in participating in a verbal exchange

3. Understand written messages in different communication situations
3.1. Select necessary information from lists or simple functional texts (brochures, menus, schedules, ads)
3.2. Extract information from multiple short texts based on several predefined or negotiated criteria/constraints
3.3. Identify information from a simple written letter/email to write an answer
3.4. Show willingness to be informed through reading

4. Write messages in everyday communication situations
4.1. Complete a form with personally identifiable information (education, interests, competences)
4.2. Write a very simple personal letter (digital version included) to express thanks or apologies
4.3. Tell a story, in short, using linkers to emphasise the chronological order
4.4. Write simple and coherent texts on specific topics of interest
4.5. Participate in the exchange of written messages

Competențele generale și specifice din programa școlară, urmărite în unitatea de învățare

1. Receptarea de mesaje orale în diverse situaţii de comunicare
1.1. Identificarea informaţiilor esenţiale din știrile prezentate la TV/materiale înregistrate, referitoare la diferite evenimente, atunci când comentariul este ilustrat prin imagini
1.2. Identificarea detaliilor din mesaje și interacţiuni pe subiecte previzibile când locutorii/interlocutorii vorbesc clar și rar
1.3. Identificarea unor elemente culturale specifice limbii studiate

2. Exprimarea orală în diverse situaţii de comunicare
2.1. Prezentarea unor planuri/unor intenţii și proiecte de viitor
2.2. Descrierea scurtă, elementară a unor activități
2.3. Inițierea, susținerea și încheierea unui dialog pe teme familiare sau de interes personal
2.4. Participarea la conversaţii în legătură cu planificarea unor activităţi
2.5. Manifestarea interesului pentru participarea la schimbul verbal

3. Receptarea de mesaje scrise în diverse situaţii de comunicare
3.1. Extragerea informaţiilor necesare din liste sau din texte funcţionale simple (pliante, meniuri, orare, reclame)
3.2. Extragerea informaţiilor din mai multe texte scurte pe baza mai multor criterii/constrângeri prestabilite sau negociate
3.3. Identificarea informaţiilor dintr-o scrisoare personală simplă/e-mail în vederea redactării unui răspuns
3.4. Manifestarea disponibilităţii pentru informare prin lectură

4. Redactarea de mesaje în diverse situaţii de comunicare
4.1. Completarea unui formular cu informaţii de identificare (educaţie, interese, competenţe)
4.2. Redactarea unei scrisori personale (inclusiv digitale) foarte simple exprimând mulțumiri sau scuze
4.3. Relatarea pe scurt a unei întâmplări utilizând cuvinte de legătură pentru a marca ordinea cronologică
4.4. Redactarea de texte simple și coerente pe teme de interes
4.5. Participarea la schimbul de mesaje scrise

8 Having fun

Vocabulary

Free time activities

1 ★ Complete the free time activities with the verbs in the box.

take	watch	spend	draw	play
~~have~~	meet	play	use	read

1 *have* a party
2 ___________ computer games
3 ___________ books or magazines
4 ___________ friends
5 ___________ films
6 ___________ time with your family
7 ___________ an instrument
8 ___________ the internet
9 ___________ pictures
10 ___________ photos

2 ★★ Choose the correct options.

1 Let's stay at home and **watch** / **use** films.
2 At weekends, I go to the shopping centre to **meet / take** my friends.
3 If you're bored, you can **use / draw** pictures.
4 My dad likes **reading / using** the internet to find information.
5 My sister **took / spent** some photos at the zoo.
6 **Having / Reading** books and magazines is a nice way to relax.
7 Barry's **using / having** a party on Friday for his birthday.

3 ★★ Complete the sentences with the correct form of the verbs in Exercise 1.

1 Yesterday I *met* my friends in the park.
2 I often ___________ the internet for my projects at school.
3 I ___________ (not) an instrument, but I'd like to learn the guitar.
4 We stayed at home and ___________ computer games because the weather was bad.
5 My friend Lucy always ___________ pictures in class.
6 I don't really like ___________ books or magazines.
7 It was my dad's birthday so we ___________ a party.
8 ___________ you ___________ a lot of photos while you were on holiday?
9 I think it's important to ___________ time with your family at the weekend.
10 When I don't want to go out, I stay at home and ___________ films on my computer.

4 ★★★ Which free time activity are they talking about? Write a sentence.

1 'This is a good one of you and Paul, you're both smiling. I'm going to put it on my blog.'
She took a photo.
2 'I've only got about 20 more pages to read. I can't wait to see what happens!'
She ___________
3 'Let's make it a surprise. Don't tell her. We'll invite all her friends.'
They ___________
4 'I've got a new one. It's cool, but I'm only on level 5 and there are 100 levels!'
He ___________
5 'OK, 11 o'clock at the door of the sports centre. Don't be late.'
They ___________
6 'I like chatting with my cousins and my mum and dad always have a great time.'
She ___________
7 'We saw a really good one last night about Sherlock Holmes, the detective.'
They ___________

Language focus 1

one/ones

1 ★ Complete the rules in the grammar table with the words in the box.

one	noun	ones	one	ones

1	We can use *one* or *ones* when we don't want to repeat a ___________ in a sentence.
2	We use ___________ to replace a singular noun.
3	My brother loves these cakes, especially this ___________ with white chocolate.
4	We use ___________ to replace a plural noun.
5	You can buy these flowers for Mum and I'll buy those ___________ for Auntie Sue.

2 ★★ Cross out the repeated words in each sentence. Write *one* or *ones* to replace them.

1 **A:** Can I have a cake, please?
B: Which ~~cake~~ *one* would you like, chocolate or strawberry?

2 I love the photos of the party, especially the photos of us dancing!

3 I don't want a small wedding. I want a big wedding!

4 **A:** Can you pass me my jacket?
B: Which jacket is it?
A: The black jacket with a grey hood.

5 **A:** Do you want a glass of water?
B: No, I've got a glass of water, thanks.

Indefinite pronouns

3 ★ Complete the rules in the grammar table with the words in the box.

negative	places	people	affirmative	things

1	We use *someone/no one/everyone/anyone* to talk about ___________.
2	We use *something/nothing/everything/anything* to talk about ___________.
3	We use *somewhere/nowhere/everywhere/anywhere* to talk about ___________.
4	We use the pronouns starting with *some-* and *every-* in ___________ sentences.
5	We use the pronouns starting with *no-* and *any-* in ___________ sentences. *I haven't got anything to do.* *I've got nothing to do.*

4 ★★ Complete the conversation with *some, any, no* or *every*.

Mum: Joe, have you seen the cat? I've looked [1] *every* where, but I can't find him.
Joe: No, I haven't! I haven't seen him [2] ___________ where this morning.
Mum: What's wrong?
Joe: I'm bored! There's [3] ___________ thing exciting to do in this place. I've got [4] ___________ where to go and [5] ___________ one to go out with.
Mum: Why not? Where are all your friends?
Joe: [6] ___________ one's busy today. Gary's gone [7] ___________ where with his parents, Josh's grandparents are visiting him, and I can't do [8] ___________ thing with Kyle because he's ill.
Mum: Well, help me find the cat, then!
Joe: OK, but wait a minute. [9] ___________ one's texting me. Maybe Gary's back home!

5 ★★★ Rewrite the sentences with the words in brackets.

1 All the students arrived in time for school. (arrive / late / for school)
Nobody arrived late for school.

2 We haven't got any food. (There's / to eat)
____

3 All the shops are closed. (There's / to go shopping)
____

4 All the people I know live in flats. (live / house)
____

5 There's no noise. (can't / hear)
____

Explore expressions with *have*

6 ★★ Match the sentence beginnings (1–6) with the sentence endings (a–f).

1 At the end of the school year, we had *b*
2 I didn't have a ___
3 When I get up in the morning, I always have ___
4 On Sunday, we went out for lunch and had ___
5 I know that if I ever have ___
6 After cycling up the hill, I had a ___

a a shower and get dressed for school.
b a party with everyone in our class.
c rest because I was very tired.
d a meal at an Indian restaurant.
e a problem, I can talk to my parents.
f good time at the party on Saturday.

Listening and vocabulary

Adjectives of feeling

1 ★ **Find eight more adjectives of feeling in the word search.**

t	i	r	e	d	g	d	t	i	i
r	h	b	m	v	y	r	e	l	n
b	m	e	b	o	u	p	s	e	t
a	f	r	a	i	d	f	u	x	e
v	g	e	r	a	s	d	r	c	r
a	n	g	r	y	g	f	p	i	e
b	t	e	a	w	k	l	r	t	s
z	o	r	s	r	e	j	i	e	t
n	y	r	s	e	w	r	s	d	e
b	o	r	e	d	t	t	e	h	d
e	e	r	d	q	d	c	d	g	k

2 ★★ **Complete the sentences with the adjectives from Exercise 1.**

1 I didn't know you were *afraid* of dogs. It's OK, he won't bite!
2 I played tennis for two hours. Now I'm feeling very __________.
3 Steve can't come to my party. I'm quite __________, I really wanted to see him.
4 Oh no, not another romantic comedy film! I'm really __________ of them. The story is always the same.
5 On my way to school, I slipped on some ice in front of all my classmates. I was really __________.
6 We're going to an amusement park tomorrow. I'm very __________. I love them!
7 I can't believe Caroline can play three instruments. I'm really __________.
8 Alan borrowed €20 from me and he hasn't paid me back. I'm really __________ with him.
9 My dad loves reading about science. He's really __________ in it.

Listening

3 ★★ **Listen to Grace and Karla talking about April Fool's Day. What happened in their class?**

4 ★★★ **Circle the correct option.**

1 They played a joke on their biology / history teacher.
2 They looked **in books / on the internet** for April Fool's jokes.
3 They made it look like there was a murder in **the classroom / the main hall**.
4 They prepared it at **lunch time / break time.**
5 They waited for the teacher to **come in / leave the classroom**.
6 The teacher looked **worried / angry**.
7 The teacher **told / didn't tell** the class an April Fool's joke.

Language focus 2

too + adjective

1 ★ **Circle the correct words in the grammar table.**

> We use *too* + adjective when we want to say something is [1]**more / less** than we want or need it to be. Its meaning is usually [2]**affirmative / negative**.

2 ★★ **Put the words in order to make sentences.**

1 her / too / I / talk / to / was / to / embarrassed
I was too embarrassed to talk to her.
2 surprised / anything / Noel / say / was / too / to
____
3 me / call / was / too / to / upset / Adam
____
4 is / to / bag / too / carry / This / heavy
____
5 says / get married / young / I'm / mum / too / My / to
____
6 small / too / everything / is / cardboard box / to / carry / This
____

(not) adjective + *enough*

3 ★ **Circle the correct words in the grammar table.**

> *Enough* always comes [1]**before / after** an adjective. We use it to say that we have [2]**less than / as much as / more than** we want or need.

4 ★★ **Complete the sentences with the adjectives in the box.**

warm	cool	tall	~~old~~	fast	strong

1 I'm not *old* enough to learn to drive. I'm only 13.
2 This plastic bag is not __________ enough to hold all these vegetables.
3 Do you think the tea is __________ enough to drink now?
4 I hate my computer! It's not __________ enough to play videos on the internet.
5 If the room is not __________ enough, I can give you a blanket.

6 Am I __________ enough to play basketball?

5 ★★★ **Rewrite the sentences with the opposite adjectives and *too* or *enough*.**

1 You were too late to see the start of the football match.
You weren't early enough to see the start of the football match.
2 This work is too bad to pass the exam.
____
3 My flat isn't big enough for a party.
____
4 We're too young to watch this film.
____
5 He was too weak to hold the books.
____

Explore making nouns from verbs

6 ★★ **Complete the second sentence so it has a similar meaning to the first.**

1 It's easy to send photos with this mobile phone.
Sending photos is easy with this mobile phone.
2 It's great fun to go to the park.
__________ to the park is great fun.
3 It's better to swim in the sea than in a pool.
__________ in the sea is better than in a pool.
4 I feel excited when I go out on Friday nights.
__________ out on Friday nights makes me feel excited.
5 It feels great to have a shower after doing sport.
__________ a shower after doing sport feels great.

Reading

1 ★ **Read the text about different amusement parks. Which has one of the highest roller coasters in the world?**

A fun day out

The first amusement parks opened in the USA in the 1870s, and the first **roller coaster** appeared in 1884. Now amusement parks are popular all over the world, but they're not all the same. Here are a few examples from different parts of the world.

Crocosaurus Cove, Darwin, Australia

This **aquarium** and theme park has big and small crocodiles and you can stand very close to them. There are lots of other attractions, too. You can have your photo taken with a baby "croc" or you can feed the snakes and crocodiles.

Universal Studios, Singapore

This theme park is small but exciting! For many people the best **ride** in the park is the *Transformers*. Visitors sit in a small car and go on a fantastic 3D **battle**. Modern technology creates some very real fire, water and smoke effects. For people who don't like rides, there's also the beach, an aquarium and other attractions based on popular films.

Window of the World, Shenzhen, China

This theme park has **replicas** of many famous **monuments** from around the world, including the Eiffel Tower (one third of the size of the real one), the Pyramids of Giza, the Colosseum in Rome, Niagara Falls and the Grand Canyon! There are also cultural events from around the world, and indoor water and ski parks.

Six Flags Magic Mountain, California

This amusement park is famous for its roller coasters! It has 18, the most in the world, including one of the tallest in the world! But if you're afraid of roller coasters, Six Flags also has themed areas with concerts, shows, games and over a hundred other rides. It's very near Hollywood so it has appeared in a lot of famous films and TV series. Some of the rides are themed, e.g. *Batman*, *Superman: Escape from Krypton* and others.

2 ★★ **Complete the definitions with the words in bold in the text.**

1 A *replica* is a copy of something.
2 A ___________ is a very fast, small train at an amusement park.
3 A machine in an amusement park that people go on is called a ___________.
4 A ___________ is an important building or place that many people know or have visited.
5 An ___________ is a place where you go to see fish and other sea animals.
6 A fight between two groups of people is a ___________.

3 ★★ **Read the text again. Match the parks with the sentences. Write *CC* for Crocosaurus Cove, *U* for Universal, *WW* for Window of the World, and *SF* for Six Flags.**

1 *U* has a ride with great special effects.
2 ___ has very dangerous animals.
3 ___ has the world record for something.
4 ___ includes attractions for people who like cinema.
5 ___ takes you on a type of international tour.
6 ___ has animals you can see or touch.
7 ___ has a place where you can go swimming.

4 ★★ **Have you or your friends been to an amusement park? What did you do there? Write at least five sentences.**

____
____
____
____
____
____
____
____

Writing

An email invitation to a friend

1 Read Andy's email. What is he going to do on his birthday and where is he going to do it?

YourMAIL ⊕ New Reply | ▾ Delete Junk | ▾

Hi Nina,

I haven't heard from you for ages. How are things at your new school? Is [1]**it** strict?

I'm writing to invite you to my birthday party! I didn't want a big [2]**one** so Mum suggested a day out with a few friends. I've decided to try a new sport called power kiting. Have you heard of [3]**it**? It's a combination of skateboarding (I know you love [4]**that** ☺) and flying a kite. What do you think?

Anyway, [5]**it**'s on Saturday 16 May. Martin and Alex are coming. We're meeting at my house at 10:30 a.m. to go together. There's a fast food restaurant next to the beach, so we can have lunch [6]**there**. Hope you can come!

Write back soon,
Andy

2 Read the email again. Answer the questions.

1. What does Andy invite Nina to?
2. What is power kiting?
3. When is he going power kiting?
4. Who is going with him?
5. Where are they meeting?
6. Where are they going to have lunch?

Useful language Referencing words

3 Look back at Andy's email. What do the words in bold (1–6) refer to?

1. *Nina's new school*
2. ______
3. ______
4. ______
5. ______
6. ______

4 Complete the sentences with the correct referencing words.

1. Where's John? I can't find *him* and I've called ______ three times.
2. I'd like you to come to the aquarium with me. Would you like ______?
3. An amusement park? What can you do ______?
4. There are two roller coasters and I want to go on the ______ called the 'Flying Fish'.
5. I sent an invitation to everyone in my class and ______ all said ______'d come.
6. There are a lot rides so I think we should go on the ______ that we all like.

5 Match the descriptions of the activities with the places in the box.

aquarium	water park	~~ice-skating centre~~
adventure sports centre	zoo	

1. It'll be cold and you'll need warm socks for the skates. *ice-skating centre*
2. They're going to tell us about the animals and we can feed some of the birds. ______
3. I don't think they'll let us swim with the dolphins, but we can touch them. ______
4. We're going to go down some huge water slides. Bring a towel! ______
5. We can go on the climbing wall and go power kiting too. ______

Writing

6 Complete the sentences with the present continuous form of the verbs in brackets.

1 We*'re meeting* (meet) at Gina's house at 2 o'clock.
2 Tom and I ___________ (have) lunch at the water park.
3 We ___________ (take) the bus to the zoo from the city centre.
4 Patricia and Nicola ___________ (come) and we ___________ (go) skating.
5 Jan and I ___________ (leave) at 3 o'clock so let's meet at the door.

WRITING TIP

Make it better! ✓✓✓
Finish your email invitation by saying how excited you are that your friend will come.
I'm really looking forward to seeing you.

7 Which sentence does not say that you are excited?

1 Hope you can come!
2 It'll be great if you can come too!
3 I'm sure we'll have a fantastic time together!
4 I'm not sure what we're going to do.
5 I really hope you can join us.

8 Order the things Andy does in his email (1–6).

finishes the email
gives the reason for the celebration
explains arrangements
invites Nina
~~asks Nina about her life~~
explains the activity

1 *asks Nina about her life*
2 ___________
3 ___________
4 ___________
5 ___________
6 ___________

PLAN

9 You are going to write an email to a friend inviting them to a day out on your birthday. Choose one of the ideas below or your own. Then use the information in Exercise 8 and make notes.

a An ice-skating centre
b A water park
c An adventure sports centre

WRITE

10 Write the email invitation. Look at page 103 of the Student's Book to help you.

____
____
____
____
____
____
____
____
____
____
____
____

CHECK

11 Check your writing. Can you say YES to these questions?

- Did you use the ideas in Exercise 8?
- Did you use referencing words correctly?
- Did you give a description of the activities?
- Did you talk about arrangements you've made with other people?
- Did you say you are excited about the plans?

Do you need to write a second draft?

8 Review

Vocabulary
Free time activities

1 Match the verbs (1–10) and the nouns (a–j).

1	spend	a	an instrument
2	play	b	the internet
3	read	c	a party
4	use	d	computer games
5	meet	e	photos
6	play	f	films
7	have	g	books or magazines
8	draw	h	time with your family
9	take	i	friends
10	watch	j	pictures

Total: 9

Adjectives of feeling

2 Match the sentence halves.

1 I'm angry *i*
2 I'm excited ___
3 I'm afraid ___
4 I'm upset ___
5 I'm embarrassed ___
6 I'm bored ___
7 I'm tired ___
8 I'm interested ___
9 I'm surprised ___

a because the teacher told everyone I didn't do my homework.
b of spiders. I hate them!
c because I couldn't sleep last night.
d in learning how to speak Chinese.
e because my best friend is moving away.
f about going to the ballet this weekend.
g that my grandmother is on Facebook!
h with these computer games. They're all the same.
i with my sister. She broke my mobile phone!

Total: 8

Language focus
one/ones

3 Complete the sentences with *one* or *ones*.

1 I don't usually like parties, but that was a good *one*.
2 These birthday cards are really expensive. Have you got any cheaper ___________?
3 Which do you like best, the orange skirt or the red ___________?
4 She wants some new trainers for her birthday. She doesn't like her old ___________.

Total: 3

Indefinite pronouns

4 Choose the correct options.

1 Everything / (Everyone) was having a good time at the party.
2 There's **nowhere / nothing** to do here. I'm bored.
3 There's **someone / something** in my eye. It really hurts!
4 **Everywhere / Everyone** I look, I can see books and paper.
5 I've got **nothing / something** to tell you, I'm getting married!
6 We always do **anything / something** on my birthday, we never stay at home.
7 Did you get Mum **anything / anyone** for Mother's Day?

Total: 6

too + adjective

5 Complete the sentences with the adjectives below and *too*.

expensive tired cold dangerous young ~~late~~ slow

1 Go to sleep. It's *too late* to play computer games.
2 I think it's ___________ to go out without your coat. It's snowing outside!
3 You're ___________ to play another game of tennis. Go and lie down!
4 I was ___________ to catch the ball and it hit me in the face!
5 I'd like to try surfing, but my mum says it's ___________.
6 My brother wants to buy this mobile phone, but it's ___________.
7 My mum says I'm ___________ to leave school so I have to study for another year.

Total: 6

(*not*) adjective + *enough*

6 Write *enough* in the correct place in the sentences.

1 One plastic bag wasn't big *enough* for all the shopping so we bought another one.
2 Are you old to learn to drive in your country?
3 He's not strong to carry that.
4 My English isn't good to pass the exam.
5 It's not quiet to study in the library.
6 Can you run fast to win the race?

Total: 5

Language builder

7 Complete the text with the correct options.

Jan: We [1]__________ to WaveWorld next weekend. Do you want to come with us?
Pete: Yes, please! I [2]__________ there.
Jan: It's a lot of fun! We [3]__________ there last year. There are [4]__________ really good water slides and [5]__________ big wave pool. I think it's [6]__________ than Watercity.
Pete: It sounds good! I [7]__________ to go with you. I think it [8]__________ be sunny on Saturday?
Jan: Yes, I hope so. And you won't be bored. There's always [9]__________ to do because they've got lots of different rides.
Pete: I see. Which ride is [10]__________?
Jan: I think the Bungee Jump is the best. I'll try that next time!

1 (a) are going **b** go **c** will go
2 **a** didn't go **b** have never been **c** didn't went
3 **a** have gone **b** going **c** went
4 **a** much **b** some **c** a lot
5 **a** a **b** some **c** many
6 **a** best **b** better **c** good
7 **a** like **b** don't like **c** 'd like
8 **a** must **b** can **c** will
9 **a** somebody **b** something **c** nothing
10 **a** the exciting **b** the most exciting **c** the more exciting

Total: 9

Vocabulary builder

8 Circle the correct options.

1 Most people __________ money when they want to buy a house or a car.
(a) borrow **b** buy **c** earn
2 I'm __________ about going to the concert on Saturday.
a sad **b** angry **c** excited
3 Nina wants to __________ to study Art and Design.
a get a job **b** leave school **c** go to university
4 The road is icy. Don't __________.
a slip **b** hurt **c** break
5 This knife is really sharp. Don't __________ your finger.
a cut **b** bang **c** burn
6 Tony banged his arm on the door and hurt his __________.
a ankle **b** knee **c** elbow
7 You can buy cereal in a cardboard __________.
a box **b** tin **c** jar
8 __________ your coat because it's cold.
a Take off **b** Get up **c** Put on
9 We usually buy water in a plastic __________.
a jar **b** bottle **c** box
10 Some people dream __________ having a lot of money.
a with **b** about **c** on
11 Your __________ is between your head and your arm.
a chest **b** shoulder **c** back
12 Haley is __________ because her sister lost her favourite T-shirt.
a tired **b** bored **c** angry

Total: 11

Speaking

9 Put the sentences in the correct order to make a conversation.

___ **A:** It's too cold and I'd rather go somewhere more interesting.
___ **A:** That's a great idea!
1 **A:** What shall we do on Saturday?
___ **B:** Let's go to the park. We can take our bikes.
___ **B:** Why don't we meet at ten outside the front entrance?
___ **B:** OK. How about going to the aquarium?

Total: 5

Total: 62

Get it right! Unit 8

Indefinite pronouns

Remember that:

- we use singular verbs with indefinite pronouns.
  ✓ ***Everyone** in my family **speaks** English.*
  ✗ ~~Everyone in my family speak English.~~
- ***nothing***, ***nowhere***, and ***no one*** are negative. You do not need to make the sentence negative.
  ✓ ***There is nothing** to do here at the weekend.*
  ✗ ~~There isn't nothing to do here at the weekend.~~

1 Correct the sentences.

1 I don't have ~~nothing~~ *anything* to do on Friday night.
2 There isn't nowhere to go in this town.
3 He explained, but I didn't understand nothing.
4 I hope everything are OK.
5 You don't have to invite nobody to come with you.

too + adjective and (*not*) + adjective + *enough*

Remember that:

- we use ***too*** + adjective to describe something. We never use *too much* + adjective.
  ✓ *I am too tired to go out tonight.*
  ✗ ~~I am too much tired to go out tonight.~~
- we use ***not*** and ***too*** <u>before</u> the adjective and ***enough*** <u>after</u> the adjective.
  ✓ *He's **not old enough** to drive.*
  ✗ ~~He's not enough old to drive.~~
- Be careful not to confuse ***too*** and ***to***.
  ✓ *I am **too** tired **to** go out tonight.*
  ✗ ~~I am to tired to go out tonight.~~

2 Are the sentences correct? Correct the incorrect sentences.

1 The weather wasn't enough good to have a picnic.
The weather wasn't good enough to have a picnic.
2 It's too much hot to study. Please open the window.
____
3 Travelling by train is too much expensive and I'm not enough old to drive.
____
4 The soup wasn't hot enough and the pizza was too cold.
____
5 I'm tired too much to go out tonight.
____

Adjectives of feeling

Remember that:

- we use adjectives ending in ***-ed*** to say how a person feels.
  ✓ *I play games on my phone when I'm **bored**.*
  ✗ ~~I play games on my phone when I'm boring.~~
- we use adjectives ending in ***-ing*** to describe the things that cause the feelings.
  ✓ *It was an **exciting** film.* ✗ ~~It was an excited film.~~

3 Choose correct options.

1 I was really **surprised** (circled) / **surprising** by his answer.
2 They're very **interesting / interested** in the history of the city.
3 This TV programme is **bored / boring**.
4 I'm very **excited / exciting** about the wedding.
5 I'm not going out. I'm too **tired / tiring**.

Spell it right! Difficult words

These words from the Student's Book are in the top 12 words that A2 students spell incorrectly most often. Remember to spell them correctly.

because	beautiful	tomorrow
comfortable	mobile	interesting
competition	address	birthday
hello		

4 <u>Underline</u> and correct the mistake in each sentence.

1 My brother is unhealthy <u>becouse</u> he doesn't do sport. *because*
2 We stayed at a hotel in a beatiful forest in Wales. ________
3 We're going to watch a film in class tomorow. ________
4 The ice bed was more confortable than their bed at home. ________
5 I'm saving for a new mobil phone. ________
6 Elsa saw some intresting things at the museum yesterday. ________
7 Alice, you're the winner of our photography competion. ________
8 Please write your adress on this piece of paper. ________
9 I'm going to bake a cake for my brother's brithday. ________
10 They never smile or say hellow. ________

9 Reading for pleasure

General and specific competences from the curriculum explored in the unit

1. Understand oral messages in different communication situations
1.1. Identify essential information from the news presented on TV/recorded materials related to different events, when the comment is illustrated by pictures
1.2. Identify details from messages and interactions on predictable topics, when the speakers/interlocutors talk clearly and slowly
1.3. Identify specific aspects of the culture of the language studied

2. Speak in different communication situations
2.1. Present plans, intentions and future projects
2.2. Give a short and simple presentation on activities
2.3. Initiate, continue and finish a dialogue on familiar or personal interest topics
2.4. Participate in conversations related to planning activities
2.5. Show interest in participating in a verbal exchange

3. Understand written messages in different communication situations
3.1. Select necessary information from lists or simple functional texts (brochures, menus, schedules, ads)
3.2. Extract information from multiple short texts based on several predefined or negotiated criteria/constraints
3.3. Identify information from a simple written letter/email to write an answer
3.4. Show willingness to be informed through reading

4. Write messages in everyday communication situations
4.1. Complete a form with personally identifiable information (education, interests, competences)
4.2. Write a very simple personal letter (digital version included) to express thanks or apologies
4.3. Tell a story, in short, using linkers to emphasise the chronological order
4.4. Write simple and coherent texts on specific topics of interest
4.5. Participate in the exchange of written messages

Competenţele generale şi specifice din programa şcolară, urmărite în unitatea de învăţare

1. Receptarea de mesaje orale în diverse situaţii de comunicare
1.1. Identificarea informaţiilor esenţiale din ştirile prezentate la TV/materiale înregistrate, referitoare la diferite evenimente, atunci când comentariul este ilustrat prin imagini
1.2. Identificarea detaliilor din mesaje şi interacţiuni pe subiecte previzibile când locutorii/interlocutorii vorbesc clar şi rar
1.3. Identificarea unor elemente culturale specifice limbii studiate

2. Exprimarea orală în diverse situaţii de comunicare
2.1. Prezentarea unor planuri/unor intenţii şi proiecte de viitor
2.2. Descrierea scurtă, elementară a unor activităţi
2.3. Iniţierea, susţinerea şi încheierea unui dialog pe teme familiare sau de interes personal
2.4. Participarea la conversaţii în legătură cu planificarea unor activităţi
2.5. Manifestarea interesului pentru participarea la schimbul verbal

3. Receptarea de mesaje scrise în diverse situaţii de comunicare
3.1. Extragerea informaţiilor necesare din liste sau din texte funcţionale simple (pliante, meniuri, orare, reclame)
3.2. Extragerea informaţiilor din mai multe texte scurte pe baza mai multor criterii/constrângeri prestabilite sau negociate
3.3. Identificarea informaţiilor dintr-o scrisoare personală simplă/e-mail în vederea redactării unui răspuns
3.4. Manifestarea disponibilităţii pentru informare prin lectură

4. Redactarea de mesaje în diverse situaţii de comunicare
4.1. Completarea unui formular cu informaţii de identificare (educaţie, interese, competenţe)
4.2. Redactarea unei scrisori personale (inclusiv digitale) foarte simple exprimând mulţumiri sau scuze
4.3. Relatarea pe scurt a unei întâmplări utilizând cuvinte de legătură pentru a marca ordinea cronologică
4.4. Redactarea de texte simple şi coerente pe teme de interes
4.5. Participarea la schimbul de mesaje scrise

A Reading for pleasure

1 ★ **Read text A quickly. Find the name of the bird in the photo.**

2 ★★ **Read text A again and put sentences a–f in the correct order.**

a The bird began to sing on the wall. ___

b Mary ran down the garden path. _1_

c She opened the door and went inside. ___

d She saw the bird again. ___

e She spoke to the bird. ___

f She saw an old door in the wall. ___

A

Adapted from *The Secret Garden* by Frances Hodgson Burnett

Mary walked around the flower garden and the fruit trees. Then <u>she</u> went to her own special path and decided to run from one end to the other. It was a long path and she ran slowly, but she soon got hot and tired. She stopped with a laugh – and then, suddenly, she saw a little bird. It was the robin! As Mary went towards him she felt the heavy key in <u>her</u> pocket.

'Yesterday you showed me where the key was,' she said. 'Today you should show me the door.'

The robin flew from his branch to the top of the wall. Then <u>he</u> opened his mouth and sang a loud, lovely song.

A breath of wind came down the path. <u>It</u> was strong enough to move the long branches of *ivy hanging from the wall. Mary jumped forward. For a moment she could see something under the leaves, something unusual.

She began to push the ivy to one side. It hung in a long curtain over the wall, and under it Mary could see wood and metal. Her heart began to jump with excitement. The robin kept singing, as if he was excited too.

It was a door which had been closed for many years. Mary put her hand in her pocket and took out the key. She put it in the keyhole. She had to use two hands to turn <u>it</u> – but yes, it turned.

And then she took a long breath. She looked behind her up the long path. No one was there. She held back the curtain of ivy and pushed the door, which opened slowly … slowly. Then she slipped through the opening and shut the door behind her. She stood with her back against <u>it</u>, looking around her in amazement.

She was standing inside the secret garden.

*ivy - an evergreen plant (= one that never loses its leaves) that often grows up trees or buildings

3 ★★ **What do the <u>underlined</u> words refer to?**

1 she (line 1) _Mary_

2 her (line 4) ______

3 he (line 6) ______

4 It (line 7) ______

5 it (line 12) ______

6 it (line 15) ______

4 ★ **Look at the photo. Where does the road go to? Read Text B quickly to find the answer.**

5 ★★ **Match the underlined words in Text B with their meanings.**

1 cool — d
2 less
3 drop
4 froze
5 shoulder
6 alone
7 pale

a without other people
b a small round bit of liquid
c without much colour
d a little cold
e not as much
f the part of your body between the top of your arm and your neck
g stopped moving

6 ★★ **Are these sentences about text A or text B? Tick the correct box.**

The main character …	Text A	Text B
1 is a man who lives in a city.	☐	✓
2 has a unusual experience at night.	☐	☐
3 gets a wonderful surprise.	☐	☐
4 discovers something that was not easy to find.	☐	☐
5 becomes suddenly frightened.	☐	☐
6 doesn't want anyone to see him/her.	☐	☐
7 doesn't answer a question.	☐	☐
8 is a girl in a story for children.	☐	☐

7 ★★★ **Choose text A or text B and write about what happened next.**

- Describe what Mary saw in the garden.

OR

- Continue the conversation between the man and the woman in white.

B

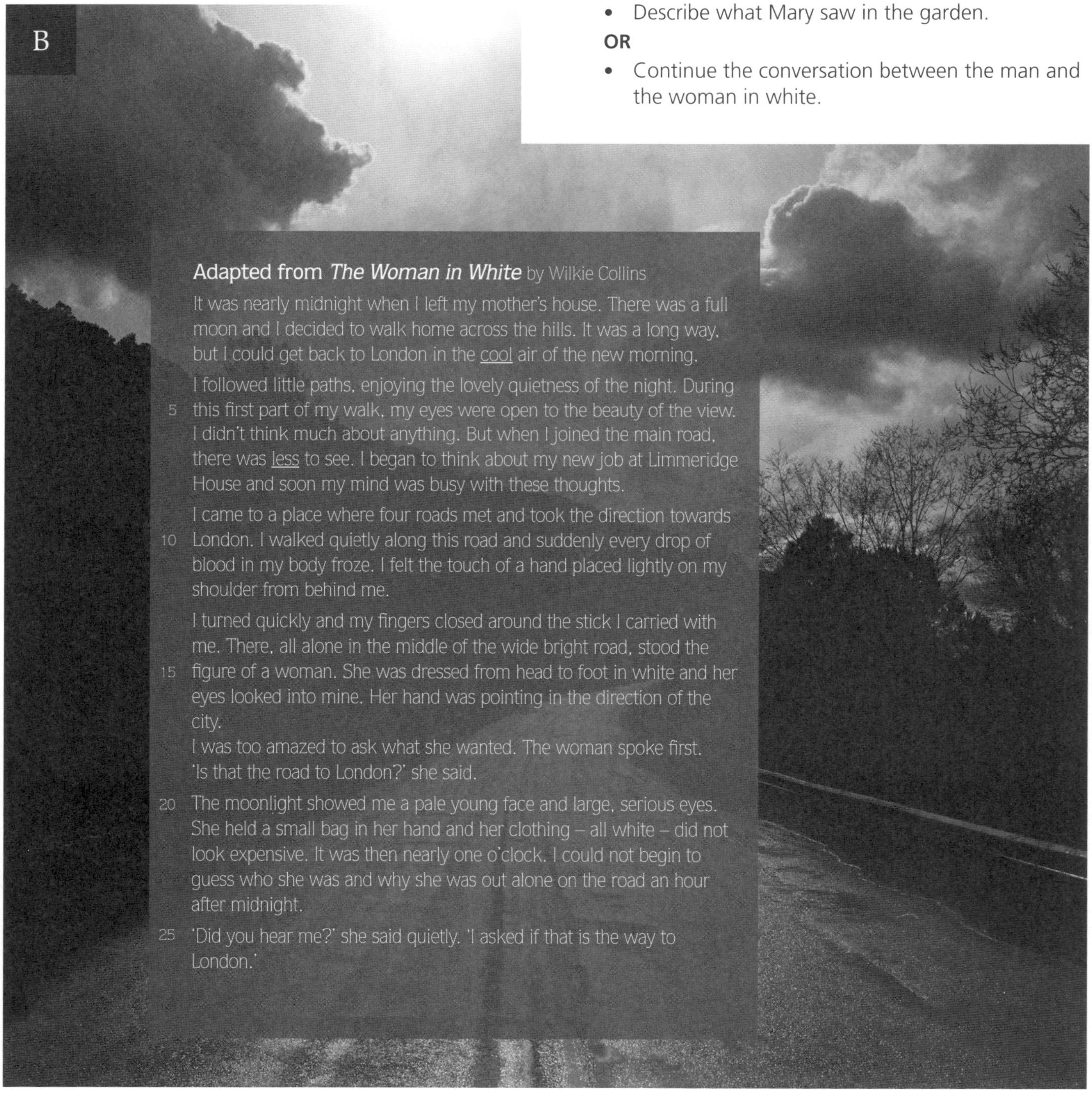

Adapted from *The Woman in White* by Wilkie Collins

It was nearly midnight when I left my mother's house. There was a full moon and I decided to walk home across the hills. It was a long way, but I could get back to London in the <u>cool</u> air of the new morning.

I followed little paths, enjoying the lovely quietness of the night. During this first part of my walk, my eyes were open to the beauty of the view. I didn't think much about anything. But when I joined the main road, there was <u>less</u> to see. I began to think about my new job at Limmeridge House and soon my mind was busy with these thoughts.

I came to a place where four roads met and took the direction towards London. I walked quietly along this road and suddenly every drop of blood in my body froze. I felt the touch of a hand placed lightly on my shoulder from behind me.

I turned quickly and my fingers closed around the stick I carried with me. There, all alone in the middle of the wide bright road, stood the figure of a woman. She was dressed from head to foot in white and her eyes looked into mine. Her hand was pointing in the direction of the city.

I was too amazed to ask what she wanted. The woman spoke first. 'Is that the road to London?' she said.

The moonlight showed me a pale young face and large, serious eyes. She held a small bag in her hand and her clothing – all white – did not look expensive. It was then nearly one o'clock. I could not begin to guess who she was and why she was out alone on the road an hour after midnight.

'Did you hear me?' she said quietly. 'I asked if that is the way to London.'

B Reading for pleasure

1 ★ Read Text A very quickly. Who is going to travel on the boat?

A

Adapted from *The Voyage* by Katherine Mansfield

The Picton boat was due to leave at half-past eleven. It was a beautiful night, **mild**, **starry** with a light wind. It was dark in the port, very dark. Fenella's father walked quickly. Beside him, her grandma walked along in her long, black coat. As well as her **luggage**, Fenella carried her grandma's umbrella. 'First **whistle**,' said her father, and at that moment they saw the Picton boat. You could see the boat in the dark night because it was covered in golden lights: it looked ready to travel among the stars, not in the cold sea. People walked along the **gangway**. First her grandma, then her father, then Fenella. They moved out of the way of the other passengers and stood under the stairs and began to say goodbye. 'There, Mother, there's your luggage!' said Fenella's father, giving Grandma another bag.

'Thank you, Frank.' 'And have you got your cabin tickets safe?' 'Yes, dear.' 'And your other tickets?' Grandma felt inside her pocket and showed him the tickets. 'That's right.' He sounded angry, but Fenella saw that he looked tired and sad. They heard the second whistle above their heads. 'You'll give my love to Father,' Fenella heard him say. Grandma was a little worried and answered, 'Of course I will, Frank. Go now. You'll be left on the boat. Go now, Frank. Go now.' 'It's alright, Mother. I've got another three minutes.' To her surprise, Fenella saw her father take off his hat. He held Grandma in his arms. Fenella turned her back on them and looked at the little green star high up on the ship. She turned round again because her father was about to leave.

'Good-bye, Fenella. Be a good girl.' Fenella held onto his coat. 'How long am I going to stay?' she **whisper**ed. He didn't look at her, but he said kindly, 'We'll see about that. Here! Where's your hand?' He gave her a **shilling**. 'That's for the journey.' A shilling! That was a lot of money. 'Am I going away **forever**?' thought Fenella. 'Father!' Fenella cried. But he was gone. He was the last person off the ship.

2 ★★ Read the text again. Complete the summary with the words in the list.

worried ~~family~~ busy realises bags light

Three members of the same ¹ *family* have arrived at a port. It's late at night and there isn't much ²________. The grandmother and granddaughter, Fenella, have some ³________ with them. When they get on the boat, it's very ⁴________. The man, Fenella's father, is ⁵________. He doesn't want to leave his mother and daughter. Fenella is very upset when her father leaves. She ⁶________ that she won't see him for a long time.

3 ★★ Look at the underlined words in the text. Match them to their definitions.

1 mild	a a bridge that people use to get on or off a ship
2 starry	b to speak very quietly so that only the person close to you can hear you
3 luggage	c a unit of money used in Britain until 1971
4 whistle	d for all time
5 gangway	e when the weather isn't very cold, or isn't as cold as usual
6 whisper	f all of the bags you take with you when you're travelling
7 shilling	g with lots of stars
8 forever	h an object you blow through to make a loud, high sound

4 ★ Look at the picture and read Text B quickly. Who is the man?

B

Adapted from *Oliver Twist* by Charles Dickens

The boys ate in a large hall. There was a table at one end with a big **saucepan** on it. One of the masters, dressed in an **apron**, served the **soup** at mealtimes. Each boy had one **bowl** of thin soup and no more – except on very special days when he also had a small piece of bread. The boys usually wanted more to eat, but they were afraid to ask. Oliver Twist and his friends were sad and hungry for three months until, one day, they decided that they couldn't continue. They had a meeting to choose a boy to ask the master for more food; they chose Oliver Twist.

The evening arrived and the boys went to the hall for **supper**. The master, in his cook's uniform, stood near the big saucepan. The boys ate the soup and then they told Oliver to go. Oliver stood up and walked to the master with his bowl and spoon in his hand. He said: 'Please, sir, I want some more.' The master looked at the small boy for a few seconds. The boys were too afraid to move. 'What!' said the master finally. 'Please, sir,' replied Oliver, 'I want some more.' The master hit Oliver on the head and held him. He shouted for Mr Bumble.

Mr Bumble ran into the meeting of the ***director**s of the **orphanage**. 'Excuse me, gentlemen! Oliver Twist has asked for more!' There was quiet. 'For more!' said one of the directors. 'Do I understand that he ate his soup and then he asked for more?' 'He did, sir,' replied Mr Bumble. After a while, the directors put Oliver into a small, dark room all alone. The next morning, they put a notice on the gate: 'Boy available. Price £5.' They didn't want Oliver at the orphanage any more.

** director - an important man at the orphanage*

5 ★★ Complete the sentences with the words in the list.

supper orphanages ~~soup~~
saucepan aprons director

1 Gazpacho is a type of *soup* that people eat in Spain.
2 The ___________ is the most important person in a company.
3 ___________ is a meal that you eat in the evening.
4 Chefs in professional kitchens usually wear ___________ at work.
5 In the past, children with no parents lived in ___________.
6 You can use a ___________ to cook food on top of a cooker.

6 ★★ Are these sentences about text A or text B? Tick the correct box.

The main character …	Text A	Text B
1 has no parents.	☐	✓
2 is going to stay with family members.	☐	☐
3 receives some money.	☐	☐
4 doesn't get enough to eat.	☐	☐
5 is sad to leave somebody they love.	☐	☐
6 gets in trouble for asking for something.	☐	☐
7 spends a night alone.	☐	☐
8 doesn't know how long they are going away for.	☐	☐

7 ★★★ Choose text A or text B and write a diary entry for the main character.

- Describe how Fenella feels on the boat journey that night.

OR

- Describe how Oliver feels when he finds out he has to leave the orphanage.

Speaking extra

General and specific competences from the curriculum explored in the unit

1. Understand oral messages in different communication situations
1.1. Identify essential information from the news presented on TV/recorded materials related to different events, when the comment is illustrated by pictures
1.2. Identify details from messages and interactions on predictable topics, when the speakers/interlocutors talk clearly and slowly
1.3. Identify specific aspects of the culture of the language studied

2. Speak in different communication situations
2.1. Present plans, intentions and future projects
2.2. Give a short and simple presentation on activities
2.3. Initiate, continue and finish a dialogue on familiar or personal interest topics
2.4. Participate in conversations related to planning activities
2.5. Show interest in participating in a verbal exchange

3. Understand written messages in different communication situations
3.1. Select necessary information from lists or simple functional texts (brochures, menus, schedules, ads)
3.2. Extract information from multiple short texts based on several predefined or negotiated criteria/constraints
3.3. Identify information from a simple written letter/email to write an answer
3.4. Show willingness to be informed through reading

4. Write messages in everyday communication situations
4.1. Complete a form with personally identifiable information (education, interests, competences)
4.2. Write a very simple personal letter (digital version included) to express thanks or apologies
4.3. Tell a story, in short, using linkers to emphasise the chronological order
4.4. Write simple and coherent texts on specific topics of interest
4.5. Participate in the exchange of written messages

Competenţele generale și specifice din programa școlară, urmărite în unitatea de învățare

1. Receptarea de mesaje orale în diverse situaţii de comunicare
1.1. Identificarea informaţiilor esenţiale din știrile prezentate la TV/materiale înregistrate, referitoare la diferite evenimente, atunci când comentariul este ilustrat prin imagini
1.2. Identificarea detaliilor din mesaje și interacţiuni pe subiecte previzibile când locutorii/interlocutorii vorbesc clar și rar
1.3. Identificarea unor elemente culturale specifice limbii studiate

2. Exprimarea orală în diverse situaţii de comunicare
2.1. Prezentarea unor planuri/unor intenţii și proiecte de viitor
2.2. Descrierea scurtă, elementară a unor activităţi
2.3. Inițierea, susținerea și încheierea unui dialog pe teme familiare sau de interes personal
2.4. Participarea la conversaţii în legătură cu planificarea unor activităţi
2.5. Manifestarea interesului pentru participarea la schimbul verbal

3. Receptarea de mesaje scrise în diverse situaţii de comunicare
3.1. Extragerea informaţiilor necesare din liste sau din texte funcţionale simple (pliante, meniuri, orare, reclame)
3.2. Extragerea informațiilor din mai multe texte scurte pe baza mai multor criterii/constrângeri prestabilite sau negociate
3.3. Identificarea informaţiilor dintr-o scrisoare personală simplă/e-mail în vederea redactării unui răspuns
3.4. Manifestarea disponibilităţii pentru informare prin lectură

4. Redactarea de mesaje în diverse situaţii de comunicare
4.1. Completarea unui formular cu informaţii de identificare (educaţie, interese, competenţe)
4.2. Redactarea unei scrisori personale (inclusiv digitale) foarte simple exprimând mulțumiri sau scuze
4.3. Relatarea pe scurt a unei întâmplări utilizând cuvinte de legătură pentru a marca ordinea cronologică
4.4. Redactarea de texte simple și coerente pe teme de interes
4.5. Participarea la schimbul de mesaje scrise

Speaking extra

Shopping

1 ★ **Put the words in order to make questions and answers from the Real talk video in the Student's Book.**

1 do / money / How / you / your / spend / ?

____

2 my / spend / food / I / money / usually / on

____

3 love / friends / shopping / going / with / my / I

____

4 friends / my / to / go / money / with / I / out / use

____

5 spend / a / tickets / lot / of / on / I / concert / money

____

2 ★★ **Listen and choose the correct answer.**

Conversation 1:

1 The girl wants to buy **a sweater** / **trainers**.

Conversation 2:

2 The boy wants to buy a **medium** / **large** T-shirt.

3 He prefers the **red** / **black** one.

Conversation 3:

4 The girl wants to buy **jeans** / **a shirt**.

5 She doesn't like the **size** / **colour**.

3 ★ **Read the conversation. Which game does Oliver buy?**

Oliver:	Excuse me, I'd [1]__________ to buy the new *MegaZoo 5* video game.
Shop assistant:	Sure, it's over there.
Oliver:	How [2]__________ is it?
Shop assistant:	It's £26.99.
Oliver:	And how much is the *Doghouse* game?
Shop assistant:	It's £45.99.
Oliver:	OK, I think I'd [3]__________ *MegaZoo 5*, then. Can I [4]__________ the game first?
Shop assistant:	Yes, it's in this machine here.
Oliver:	Thanks.
Shop assistant:	[5]__________ is it?
Oliver:	It's great! I'll [6]__________ it.

4 ★★ **Complete the conversation in Exercise 3 with the words in the box. Then listen and check.**

prefer play take much like How

Focus on pronunciation

5 ★ **How do you say these prices? Listen and repeat.**

1 £1.99 2 £15 3 £180 4 £56.99 5 £10.50

6 ★ **Listen to the conversation. What colour boots does Emily buy?**

Emily:	Excuse me, [1]__________ to a buy some boots.
Shop assistant:	Sure. What about these, or those ones over there?
Emily:	I think [2]__________ them in black.
Shop assistant:	OK, over here. Do you like these?
Emily:	Yes, they're quite cool. [3]__________ are they?
Shop assistant:	They're £65.99.
Emily:	[4]__________ them on?
Shop assistant:	Of course. [5]__________ are you?
Emily:	I'm usually a size 7.
Shop assistant:	Here you are. How are they?
Emily:	I like them, but have you got anything cheaper?
Shop assistant:	What about these? They're almost the same, but they're £45.75 and they're brown.
Emily:	Yes, they're great! I'll [6]__________ them.

7 ★★★ **Listen again and complete the conversation.**

8 ★★ **Listen again and check your answers. Then listen and repeat the conversation.**

Speaking extra

Speculating

1 ★ **Join the parts of the sentences from the Real talk video in the Student's Book.**

1 He can run faster
2 She's 20
3 She also helps
4 His family was very poor,
5 He saved his little sister

a a lot of children's charities.
b and she's an amazing dancer.
c but he worked hard and went to college.
d from a burning house.
e than anyone on the planet.

2 ★★ **Listen and choose the correct answer.**

Conversation 1:
1 The boy and girl see **someone famous** / **a famous photographer**.
Conversation 2:
2 The boy and girl are at a **museum** / **bookshop**.
3 They **agree** / **don't agree** on what the picture is.
Conversation 3:
4 They are in a **History** / **Art** class.

3 ★ **Read the conversation. Match the jobs with the people in the photos.**

dancer ___	scientist ___
musician ___	firefighter ___

Boy: So what do we have to do?
Girl: You never listen, do you? We have to look at these photos and decide what jobs they do.
Boy: Just by looking at the photos.
Girl: Yes. So what do you [1]___________ he is?
Boy: Well, he [2]___________ very strong … and brave, I think. So a firefighter, something like that.
Girl: Yeah, I agree. This guy looks very serious, but he's got a friendly face. He [3]___________ be an artist.
Boy: Yes, but look at the way he's standing. I [4]___________ he's a dancer.
Girl: Oh yeah. You're right. What about this woman?
Boy: I'm not [5]___________.
Girl: Well, she's wearing a white coat so could be either a scientist or a nurse.
Boy: That's [6]___________.
Girl: She [7]___________ works in a laboratory so she's a scientist.
Boy: Right. What about this woman?
Girl: I reckon she's a musician.
Boy: OK, write it down. Come on, let's check our answers.

4 ★★ **Complete the conversation in Exercise 3 with the words in the box. Then listen and check.**

reckon	possible	looks	think
definitely	could	sure	

Focus on pronunciation

5 ★ **Listen to the sentences. Do they go up or down? Listen and repeat.**

1 I'm not sure.
2 That's possible.
3 She could be a vet.
4 I reckon she's an artist.

6 ★ **Listen to the conversation. Whose phone is it?**

Mark: Look! A mobile phone.
Olivia: Oh yeah, whose [1]___________?
Mark: I'm [2]___________. It's [3]___________ someone from our class because it's in our classroom.
Olivia: [4]___________ very new. Do you think it's the teacher's phone?
Mark: [5]___________. [6]___________ it's a student's phone. Look at the photo here.
Olivia: Oh yeah. She's definitely not in our class.
Mark: [7]___________ someone's sister or cousin.
Olivia: You're right. Hold on. [8]___________ it's Vanessa's – I've seen Vanessa with that dress on so that could be her sister.
Mark: Right, let's go and find her.

7 ★★★ **Listen again and complete the conversation.**

Speaking extra

Asking for and offering help

1 ★ **Complete the sentences from the Real talk video in the Student's Book with the words in the box.**

garden	quieter	expensive	space	rooms	light

1 They're usually bigger so there's more ____________.
2 I think houses because they can be ____________.
3 Flats are small and they sometimes don't get much ____________.
4 It has a lot of ____________ and it's really comfortable.
5 There isn't usually a ____________ with a flat.
6 Houses near the centre of big cities are really ____________.

2 ★★ **Listen and answer the questions.**

Conversation 1:
1 How does the boy help the woman?
____

Conversation 2:
2 What did Sarah leave at school?
____
3 Where will Helen go later?
____

Conversation 3:
4 What does the boy have to do?
____
5 What does the girl want?
____

3 ★ **Read the conversation. What do Connor and Jonas put in the wardrobe?**

Connor: My mum says I should tidy my room before I go out.
Jonas: Well, she's right. I'll [1]____________ you a hand.
Connor: OK, let's see. The books shouldn't be on the floor. I should put them all up on that shelf.
Jonas: Here, [2]____________ do that. Oh look, *The Lord of the Rings*. Did you like it?
Connor: Yes, it's really good. Can you [3]____________ me a favour?
Jonas: Yes, of [4]____________.
Connor: Can you give me a [5]____________ and put this blanket in the wardrobe?
Jonas: [6]____________ I put this pillow in there as well?
Connor: Yes, please!

4 ★★ **Complete the conversation in Exercise 3 with the words in the box. Then listen and check.**

do	I'll	give	Shall	course	hand

Focus on pronunciation

5 ★ **Listen to the questions. Do they go up or down? Listen and repeat.**

1 Can you give me a hand?
2 Can you put this on the shelf?
3 Can you do me a favour?
4 Can you help me with this?

6 ★ **Listen to the conversation. What do Nick and Lisa put in the freezer?**

Nick: Come on, the computer's ready. Let's play.
Lisa: Hang on. I can't. My dad did the shopping and he wants me to put it all away.
Nick: OK, I'll give you [1]____________.
Lisa: Great. That way we'll finish sooner.
Nick: [2]____________ put the milk and cheese in the fridge?
Lisa: Yes, please!
Nick: Anything else?
Lisa: We should put the ice cream and the pizzas in the freezer.
Nick: [3]____________!
Lisa: And I need to wash all this fruit. [4]____________ me a hand?
Nick: Sure: Put it all in the sink and [5]____________.
Lisa: Oh and another thing. Can you do me [6]____________?
Nick: Sure.
Lisa: Can you start making lunch? I'm hungry!
Nick: Ha ha ha! Come on. Mario is waiting!

7 ★★★ **Listen again and complete the conversation.**

8 ★★ **Listen again and check your answers. Then listen and repeat the conversation.**

Speaking extra

Offering to help

1 ★ **Match the sentence halves from the Real talk video in the Student's Book.**

1 It was an enormous job, ___
2 A good friend doesn't have to do anything, ___
3 I'm not sad very often, but when I am ___
4 I can't always talk to my parents. ___
5 Sometimes it's hard ___

a I only want to talk to my friend.
b It's easier to talk to my friend.
c but a real friend never lies to you.
d but fun doing it all together.
e they just have to be there.

2 ★★ **Listen and choose the correct answer.**

Conversation 1:
1 The girl is sending a message to say **hello / sorry**.

Conversation 2:
2 The girl is doing a **Maths / English** problem.
3 In the end she **understands / doesn't understand**.

Conversation 3:
4 The boy is doing a **History / Art** project.
5 He needs a photo of a **ship / computer**.

3 ★ **Read the conversation. Where do Lily and Chloe look for information first?**

Lily: Hey, Chloe. Can I [1] ______________ you something?
Chloe: Yeah, sure. What's up?
Lily: It's this Social Science project. I have to write a biography of Nelson Mandela, but I'm not [2] ______________ where to start.
Chloe: He was very famous. What do you [3] ______________?
Lily: Well, where do I find out about him?
Chloe: I think you should look on the internet first. Here, [4] ______________ me help you.
Lily: Thanks. That's really nice of you!
Chloe: It's easy. [5] ______________ you have to do is look at an online encyclopaedia. Read about him and make notes of the most important moments in his life.
Lily: I'm not very good at deciding what's important.
Chloe: Don't worry. I'll give you a [6] ______________ if you like.
Lily: Great! That's really kind.

4 ★★ **Complete the conversation in Exercise 3 with the words in the box. Then listen and check.**

hand	sure	need	All	ask	let

Pronunciation focus: Linking words

5 ★ **Listen to the sentences. Which words are linked? Listen and repeat.**

1 Can I ask you something?
2 I'll give you a hand.
3 Let me show you.
4 I'm not sure how to do it.
5 What do you need?

6 ★ **Listen to the conversation. What two things does Lewis want to know?**

7 ★★★ **Listen again and complete the conversation.**

Oliver: Hi Lewis? What are you doing?
Lewis: Oh, hi Oliver. Just some homework. But I'm so tired.
Oliver: Here, [1] ______________ if you like.
Lewis: Thanks. I'm not very good at History.
Oliver: It's not that difficult. [2] ______________ is write the correct date.
Lewis: Yes, but I'm not very good at remembering dates. Especially when I'm tired!
Oliver: Yeah, I know. You forgot my birthday! [3] ______________?
Lewis: Let's see. When did the Romans come to Britain?
Oliver: That's in Chapter 1 of the History book. [4] ______________.
Lewis: Thanks. Oliver, [5] ______________ something?
Oliver: Sure. What's up?
Lewis: How do I get a good night's sleep?
Oliver: You have to feel relaxed before you go to sleep.
Lewis: OK, but [6] ______________ do that.
Oliver: Well let's finish this History quiz first. Let's see … the Romans in Britain … Lewis? … Lewis?

8 ★★ **Listen again and check your answers. Then listen and repeat the conversation.**

Speaking extra

UNIT 5

Asking for and giving instructions

1 ★ **Match the sentence halves from the Real talk video in the Student's Book.**

1 I don't have a phone
2 It's more important to my mum
3 It's not really important to me.
4 I use it for the games and the apps
5 My mum tells me to take it with me
a so she can call me any time she wants.
b and I watch my favourite TV programmes on it.
c whenever I go out.
d so it's not important to me at all.
e I usually leave it at home.

2 ★★ **Listen and answer the questions.**

Conversation 1:

1 What does the girl want to see?

____

Conversation 2:

2 What does the girl need to do to get on to the website?

____

3 How does she start playing?

____

Conversation 3:

4 What are they trying to do?

____

3 ★ **Read the conversation. What does Daniel teach his granddad to do on the tablet?**

Granddad: That looks exciting. What is it?
Daniel: It's a tablet. It's a kind of computer.
Granddad: Oh, I see. How does it [1]__________?
Daniel: It's easy. [2]__________, you need to press the button on the top.
Granddad: This one?
Daniel: Yes, [3]__________ it. Now, if you swipe your finger across the touchscreen, it'll turn on the apps.
Granddad: Apps?
Daniel: Yes, look, you just [4]__________ to touch one with your finger.
Granddad: Oh but, what is it?
Daniel: It's a game. It's called *Dogs in Space*.
Granddad: Oh no! How do I turn the music down?
Daniel: Find the button on the side.
Granddad: OK, [5]__________ it is.
Daniel: Then press it a few times.
Granddad: So [6]__________ do I stop it?
Daniel: Press the button at the top again.
Granddad: Oh, what's that noise?
Daniel: I just got an email.

4 ★★ **Complete the conversation in Exercise 3 with the words in the box. Then listen and check your answers.**

have	here	work	how	that's	First

Focus on pronunciation

5 ★ **Listen to the instructions. Do they go up or down? Which instruction goes down? Listen and repeat.**

1 First, click on this icon.
2 Now, look for the name of the person.
3 Now, you have to scroll down the list.
4 Then, you click on the name.
5 And just click on the green button.

6 ★ **Listen to the conversation. Why does Hugh's dad put his hand on the screen?**

Dad: I want to get on this social network. How [1]__________?
Hugh: Let's see. First, you [2]__________ create a profile.
Dad: Err … a profile. OK, [3]__________ do that?
Hugh: Click here and put in your name and all your information.
Dad: All this?
Hugh: No. You only have to put in the things with the red stars: your name, your email and a password. Now, scroll down and just click on 'Create Profile'.
Dad: Oh, I see. [4]__________?
Hugh: Yes! That's it. If you click here, you'll get an email.
Dad: OK, here it is. It says 'confirm your profile'. How do I confirm my profile?
Hugh: Just click on the link in the email.
Dad: I see! Thanks!
Hugh: And [5]__________ put your hand on the screen and say 'Hello', your friends will say 'Hello' too.
Dad: OK … 'Hello?'
Hugh: Haha! Very good, Dad, but you don't really have to do that!
Dad: Hey!

7 ★★★ **Listen again and complete the conversation.**

8 ★★ **Listen again and check your answers. Then listen and repeat the conversation.**

Speaking extra

Agreeing and disagreeing

1 ★ **Put the words in order to make sentences from the Real talk video in the Student's Book.**

1 know / yet / don't / I / going / what / I'm / to do

____

2 go / to / and / Chinese / I'm / going / to / university / study

____

3 player / going / be / a / I'm / football / to / professional

____

4 around / I'm / motorcycle / going / world / to / buy / a / ride / and / the

____

2 ★★ **Listen and answer the questions.**

Conversation 1:

1 What does the girl think about education?

____

Conversation 2:

2 Does the boy agree with the girl?

____

3 Which word does he use to describe homework?

____

Conversation 3:

4 What is the topic of their discussion?

____

3 ★ **Read the conversation. How many statements do Alex and Julie discuss?**

Alex: OK, I want you to give me your opinion about some different topics.
Julie: Sure. What topics?
Alex: Well, I have some statements about young people's lives and I need you to tell me if you agree or disagree with them.
Julie: OK. Go on then.
Alex: Let's see, first statement: Young people should get married later, for example, after university or when they have a job. Do you [1]__________?
Julie: I'm not [2]__________. I think young people should get married when they want or when they're old enough to get married in their country.
Alex: OK, next one: Too many young people go to university. What's your [3]__________?
Julie: No, I [4]__________. I think young people should be able to continue their studies when they leave school if they want to.
Alex: I agree [5]__________ you. And here's the last statement: Going to university helps you get a better job.
Julie: Absolutely! Young people who go to university can get better jobs because they know more things.
Alex: Yes, I [6]__________ you're right. But they should be able to get a job when they leave school if that's what they want to do.

4 ★★ **Complete the conversation in Exercise 3 with the words in the box. Then listen and check.**

with	agree	disagree	suppose	sure	opinion

Focus on pronunciation

5 ★ **Listen. Do the words and phrases go up or down? Listen and repeat.**

1 Absolutely.
2 I agree with you.
3 I suppose you're right.
4 Maybe, but I also think it's difficult.
5 I disagree.

6 ★ **Listen to the conversation. Where is Jessica going?**

Reporter: Excuse me! Can you give us five minutes? We'd like to know your opinion on some different topics.
Jessica: OK. What are the topics?
Reporter: Well, here's the first one: Life is more difficult now than it was for your parents. Do [1]__________?
Jessica: No, [2]__________. I think life is easier now, especially because of technology.
Reporter: OK. [3]__________ think life will be easier in the future than it is now?
Jessica: Maybe, but I [4]__________ we'll have a lot of problems … especially with the environment.
Reporter: Thanks. Next one: We'll probably live on other planets in the future. What's [5]__________?
Jessica: [6]__________! There are too many of us here on Earth!
Reporter: [7]__________ you're right. But where would we go?
Jessica: I don't know, but right now, I'm going home.
Reporter: Oh, yes, thanks for your time. Bye!

7 ★★★ **Listen again and complete the conversation.**

Speaking extra

Reacting to news

1 ★ **Match the sentence halves from the Real talk video in the Student's Book.**

1 I fell out of a tree and
2 I've broken my leg twice,
3 I cut my hand
4 I've sprained my wrists
a a lot of times playing volleyball.
b on a broken glass last week and it still hurts.
c but I can still run faster than all my friends.
d sprained my ankle when I was five.

2 ★★ **Listen and answer the questions.**

Conversation 1:
1 What happened to David last week?
____

Conversation 2:
2 What's wrong with Lisa?
____

Conversation 3:
3 Where did Charlie go on holiday?
____
4 What part of her body did Anne burn?
____

3 ★ **Read the conversation. Did something good happen to Liam or Abby?**

Abby: Hi, Liam, how's it [1]__________?
Liam: Fine thanks, Abby. How about you?
Abby: Yeah, not bad. I've got a place at university. I'm going to study Physics.
Liam: Well done! That's [2]__________.
Abby: Thanks. I'm really excited. What have you been [3]__________ to?
Liam: Well, I cut my knee while I was playing football at school. Look!
Abby: Oh no! How did you do that?
Liam: I don't know really – I fell over and another boy kicked me with his boot. When I got home, I couldn't move my leg.
Abby: What a [4]__________! When did it happen?
Liam: Last Monday. It's getting better now, but I can't play football for a few weeks.
Abby: I'm sorry to [5]__________ that.
Liam: So, tell me about your new university …

4 ★★ **Complete the conversation in Exercise 3 with the words in the box. Then listen and check your answers.**

up	shame	fantastic	hear	going

Focus on pronunciation

5 ★ **Listen. Do the phrases go up or down? Listen and repeat.**

1 Oh no!
2 What a shame!
3 I'm sorry to hear that!
4 How amazing!
5 That's fantastic!

6 ★ **Listen to the conversation. Why can't Matthew go to London?**

Lucy: Hi, Matthew, [1]__________?
Matthew: Oh, hi, Lucy, fine thanks. How about you?
Lucy: Not bad, yeah. I've just been in that shop over there. I wanted to try on some dresses for a wedding.
Matthew: [2]__________! Are you getting married?
Lucy: No! It's my brother. He's getting married in June … in London.
Matthew: In London? [3]__________!
Lucy: So … em, Matthew, [4]__________?
Matthew: Not a lot really. Studying, you know. I didn't pass my Maths exam so I have to do it again in June.
Lucy: [5]__________! In June?
Matthew: Yeah, I'm going to take the exam on 5 June.
Lucy: The 5th? [6]__________!
Matthew: Why?
Lucy: Well, that's the day my brother's getting married and … well, I wanted to invite you to come to London with me.
Matthew: Me? Really? Oh … sorry. I have to do my Maths exam!
Lucy: Well, [7]__________, Matthew.
Matthew: Yes. Me too.

7 ★★★ **Listen again and complete the conversation.**

8 ★★ **Listen again and check your answers. Then listen and repeat the conversation.**

Speaking extra

Suggesting and responding

1 ★ **Complete the sentences from the Real talk video in the Student's Book with the verbs in the box.**

wore	celebrate	invite	took	go on	have

1 I always ___________ a big party and ___________ everyone in my class.
2 I prefer to ___________ my birthday at home with my family.
3 I usually ___________ a trip with my friends or family.
4 Everybody ___________ pink and all the food was pink too.
5 I didn't celebrate it. I ___________ an exam.

2 ★★ **Listen and answer the questions.**

Conversation 1:
1 What are they going to do on Saturday?
____

Conversation 2:
2 Why is tomorrow a special day?
____
3 What are they going to do?
____

Conversation 3:
4 What would the girl prefer to do?
____
5 What do they decide to eat?
____

3 ★ **Read the conversation. Where are Ella and Mary going? Why?**

Ella: What [1]___________ we do on Sunday?
Mary: Sunday? Why?
Ella: It's my birthday. Don't you remember?
Mary: Oh, yeah! [2]___________ have a party with everybody from our class.
Ella: OK, why not? Where?
Mary: What [3]___________ having it at your house?
Ella: My house isn't big enough. I think I'd [4]___________ go out.
Mary: OK, how about meeting everyone from school for a meal somewhere?
Ella: That's a nice [5]___________! Why [6]___________ we go to that new pizza restaurant in town?
Mary: Fantastic. I'm excited already!
Ella: OK, let's call the others.

4 ★★ **Complete the conversation in Exercise 3 with the words in the box. Then listen and check.**

don't	Let's	rather	about	idea	shall

Focus on pronunciation

5 ★ **Listen to the questions. Do they go up or down? Listen and repeat.**

1 How about having a party?
2 Let's watch a film.
3 Why don't we have a meal?
4 What about meeting some friends?
5 Where shall we go tomorrow?

6 ★ **Listen to the conversation. What will Julie do at the party?**

Mike: You know it's Dad's birthday in two weeks? He's 55.
Julie: Oh, yeah! [1]___________?
Mike: [2]___________ have a surprise party?
Julie: [3]___________! We can invite all the family and a few friends.
Mike: OK, but where shall we have it? Our house is too small.
Julie: [4]___________ calling Uncle Dave? He's got a big house and a big garden. It's big enough for about 20 people.
Mike: Yes, I'm sure he'll agree.
Julie: What about asking Mum and Auntie Jean to make some food?
Mike: OK, [5]___________? But we'll have to help them.
Julie: Help them? You know I can't cook. I think [6]___________ organise the music.
Mike: You can organise the music, but you have to talk to Uncle Dave too.
Julie: Uncle Dave loves me! I'm sure he'll say yes.

7 ★★★ **Listen again and complete the conversation.**

8 ★★ **Listen again and check your answers. Then listen and repeat the conversation.**

Language focus extra

General and specific competences from the curriculum explored in the unit

1. Understand oral messages in different communication situations
1.1. Identify essential information from the news presented on TV/recorded materials related to different events, when the comment is illustrated by pictures
1.2. Identify details from messages and interactions on predictable topics, when the speakers/interlocutors talk clearly and slowly
1.3. Identify specific aspects of the culture of the language studied

2. Speak in different communication situations
2.1. Present plans, intentions and future projects
2.2. Give a short and simple presentation on activities
2.3. Initiate, continue and finish a dialogue on familiar or personal interest topics
2.4. Participate in conversations related to planning activities
2.5. Show interest in participating in a verbal exchange

3. Understand written messages in different communication situations
3.1. Select necessary information from lists or simple functional texts (brochures, menus, schedules, ads)
3.2. Extract information from multiple short texts based on several predefined or negotiated criteria/constraints
3.3. Identify information from a simple written letter/email to write an answer
3.4. Show willingness to be informed through reading

4. Write messages in everyday communication situations
4.1. Complete a form with personally identifiable information (education, interests, competences)
4.2. Write a very simple personal letter (digital version included) to express thanks or apologies
4.3. Tell a story, in short, using linkers to emphasise the chronological order
4.4. Write simple and coherent texts on specific topics of interest
4.5. Participate in the exchange of written messages

Competenţele generale și specifice din programa școlară, urmărite în unitatea de învățare

1. Receptarea de mesaje orale în diverse situaţii de comunicare
1.1. Identificarea informaţiilor esențiale din știrile prezentate la TV/materiale înregistrate, referitoare la diferite evenimente, atunci când comentariul este ilustrat prin imagini
1.2. Identificarea detaliilor din mesaje și interacţiuni pe subiecte previzibile când locutorii/interlocutorii vorbesc clar și rar
1.3. Identificarea unor elemente culturale specifice limbii studiate

2. Exprimarea orală în diverse situaţii de comunicare
2.1. Prezentarea unor planuri/unor intenţii și proiecte de viitor
2.2. Descrierea scurtă, elementară a unor activități
2.3. Inițierea, susținerea și încheierea unui dialog pe teme familiare sau de interes personal
2.4. Participarea la conversaţii în legătură cu planificarea unor activităţi
2.5. Manifestarea interesului pentru participarea la schimbul verbal

3. Receptarea de mesaje scrise în diverse situaţii de comunicare
3.1. Extragerea informaţiilor necesare din liste sau din texte funcţionale simple (pliante, meniuri, orare, reclame)
3.2. Extragerea informațiilor din mai multe texte scurte pe baza mai multor criterii/constrângeri prestabilite sau negociate
3.3. Identificarea informaţiilor dintr-o scrisoare personală simplă/e-mail în vederea redactării unui răspuns
3.4. Manifestarea disponibilităţii pentru informare prin lectură

4. Redactarea de mesaje în diverse situaţii de comunicare
4.1. Completarea unui formular cu informaţii de identificare (educaţie, interese, competenţe)
4.2. Redactarea unei scrisori personale (inclusiv digitale) foarte simple exprimând mulțumiri sau scuze
4.3. Relatarea pe scurt a unei întâmplări utilizând cuvinte de legătură pentru a marca ordinea cronologică
4.4. Redactarea de texte simple și coerente pe teme de interes
4.5. Participarea la schimbul de mesaje scrise

Language focus extra

Subject pronouns and *be*

1 **Complete the questions with *am, is* or *are*. Then match the question with the answer.**

1 When ___*is*___ your birthday? ___*c*___
2 ________ your friends at home? ______
3 How old ________ your aunt? ______
4 What time ________ it? ______
5 ________ you from Chile? ______

a No, they aren't.
b It's 10 o'clock.
c It's on 2 June.
d No, I'm not.
e She's 48.

Possessive *'s*

2 **Add *'s* or *'* to the correct place in the sentences.**

1 Martin*'s* pencil case is black and white.
2 My best friend bike is in the sports hall.
3 My parents names are Cristina and Robbie.
4 My cousin friends are in my class.
5 My three friends books are on the floor.

there is/are + some and *any*

3 **Match the sentence halves.**

1 There isn't ___*c*___
2 Are there ______
3 There aren't ______
4 There's ______
5 Is there ______

a any orange juice in that bag?
b some water in the canteen.
c any milk on the table.
d any computers in your school library?
e any dictionaries in our classroom.

Have got + a/an

4 **Read about Rachel, Ben and Tom's things and complete the table with answers about you. Use the information to write *Yes/No* questions with *have* and short answers.**

	Rachel	Ben and Tom	You
a dog or a cat	✓	✗	______
a laptop	✗	✓	______

1 *Has Rachel got a dog or a cat?* *Yes, she has.*
2 *Has Rachel got a laptop?* ________
3 ________? ________
4 ________? ________
5 ________? ________
6 ________? ________

Present simple: affirmative and negative

5 **Write sentences with the correct form of the present simple.**

1 I / not ride / my bike to school
I don't ride my bike to school.
2 My friends / play / basketball in the school team
____
3 My teacher / go / swimming in the sea every day
____
4 We / not have / lunch at home
____
5 My dad / not work / near here
____

Present simple: questions

6 **Put the words in order to make questions and write the answers.**

1 you / Where / do / live / ?
Where do you live? I live near my school.
2 you and your friends / snowboarding / Do / go / ?
____
3 lunch / What time / you / have / do / ?
____
4 Does / mum / skiing / go / your / ?
____
5 dinner / dad / Does / TV / after / your / watch / ?
____

Adverbs of frequency

7 **Circle the correct words.**

1 I **often play / play often** volleyball in the summer.
2 My sister and I **do usually / usually do** our homework in our bedroom.
3 I **am sometimes / sometimes am** tired on Monday morning.
4 We **sometimes go / go sometimes** surfing.
5 It **is never / never is** hot in December.

UNIT 1

Language focus extra

Present continuous: affirmative and negative

1 Complete the sentences with the present continuous form of the verb in brackets.

1 Lots of people *are shopping* in the mall today. (shop)
2 I ________ for a new dress. (look)
3 My mum ________ a magazine in the cafe. (read)
4 She ________ coffee. (not drink)
5 My brother ________ a computer game. (play)
6 We ________ a lot of money. (not spend)

Present continuous: *Wh-* questions

2 Write questions using the present continuous.

1 What / you / buy
What are you buying?
2 Where / they / go
________?
3 Who / she / meet
________?
4 What / Jenny / watch
________?
5 Why / we / wait
________?
6 What / Joe / wear
________?

Present continuous: *Yes/No* questions

3 Read what Maria, Judy and Tim are doing and complete the table with answers about you. Use the information to write *Yes/No* questions and short answers in the present continuous.

	Maria	Judy and Tim	You
visit the mall	✗	✓	________
study grammar	✓	✗	________

1 *Is Maria visiting the mall*? *No*, *she isn't*.
2 ________? ________, ________.
3 ________? ________, ________.
4 ________? ________, ________.
5 ________? ________, ________.
6 ________? ________, ________.

Spelling: *-ing* form

4 Complete the chart with the *-ing* form of the verbs in the box.

~~do~~ get look make run write

Add *-ing*	Remove the *-e* and add *-ing*	Double consonant and add *-ing*
1 *doing*	3 ________	5 ________
2 ________	4 ________	6 ________

Present simple vs. continuous

5 Complete the sentences with the present simple or present continuous form of the verbs in the box.

buy not do ~~eat~~ not talk visit

1 We *are eating* pizza right now.
2 I ________ my homework at the moment.
3 They often ________ the mall on Saturdays.
4 My mum ________ books in that shop.
5 Joe ________ on his mobile right now.

(don't) want to, would(n't) like to, would prefer to, would rather/would sooner

6 Circle the correct options.

1 I don't **want** / **like** to go to school today.
2 Jack likes playing football, but he'd **want / prefer** to go swimming today.
3 Would you **want / like** to come with me?
4 I wouldn't **like / prefer** to do judo.
5 We've got Maths and English homework today. I'd **want / prefer** to do English first.
6 I'd sooner **read / to read** the novel than watch the film.
7 **Would / Will** you rather go shopping with me than clean your room?

(not) enough + noun

7 Complete the sentences with *enough* and the words in the box.

money milk ~~paper~~ chairs time

1 There isn't *enough* *paper* for everyone.
2 I'd like to buy a skateboard, but I haven't got ________ ________.
3 Sit down, everybody. Oh sorry, we haven't got ________ ________.
4 We can't go to the bookshop now. We haven't got ________ ________. It's late.
5 Have you got ________ ________ for three glasses?

Language focus extra

was/were: affirmative and negative

1 Complete the sentences with the correct form of *was* or *were*.

At school, I [1] *wasn't* (not) very good at sport, but I [2] ________ good at dancing. My friends [3] ________ all crazy about football. They [4] ________ (not) interested in dancing. I saw my first ballet when I [5] ________ 12 years old. It [6] ________ amazing!

Past simple: affirmative and negative

2 Write sentences in the past simple.

1 Tim / play / football / yesterday
Tim played football yesterday.
2 Joanna / go skiing / last winter
____
3 Gina and Tony / grow up / in Canada
____
4 We / not want / to practise the piano / last weekend
____
5 I / not play / tennis / at school / when I was little
____
6 Nicky / not win / the singing competition / last week
____

Past simple: irregular verbs

3 Write the past simple of each verb.

1 have *had*
2 make ________
3 become ________
4 write ________
5 get ________
6 see ________

Past simple: spelling

4 Complete the chart with the past simple form of each verb.

like stop dance study try ~~wait~~

Add -*ed*	Add -*d*
1 *waited*	2 ________ 3 ________
Remove the last letter and add -*ied*	**Double the last consonant and add -*ed***
4 ________ 5 ________	6 ________

was/were: questions

5 Complete the questions with the past simple of *be* and write the short answers.

1 *Were* you in judo class yesterday?
Yes, I was. ✓
2 ________ Jake good at sports at school?
________. ✓
3 ________ they in the supermarket this morning? No, ________. ✗
4 ________ he unfriendly at the party?
________. ✗

Past simple: *Wh-* questions

6 Write a question for each answer. Use the past simple.

1 'What *did you drink*?'
'I drank some lemonade.'
2 'Where ________?'
'He went to a concert.'
3 'When ________?'
'They started school at 9 a.m.'
4 'Who ________?'
'She met her sister.'

Past simple: *Yes/No* questions

7 Read what Helen, Sam and Abby did last weekend and complete the table with answers about you. Use the information to write *Yes/No* questions and short answers in the past simple. Write them in your notebook.

	Helen	Sam and Abby	You
eat pizza	✗	✓	________
go shopping	✓	✗	________

1 *Did Helen eat pizza*? *No*, *she didn't*.

used to + infinitive

8 Complete the interview with *used to* and the verbs in brackets.

Interviewer: You [1] *used to live* in a small village, but now you live in Bucharest. (live)
Old man: That's right. I grew up in Dragus. I [2] ________ it there. (like)
Interviewer: Was life hard in the past?
Old man: It was. We [3] ________ central heating and electricity, but we still enjoyed life. (not have)
Interviewer: I see. What [4] ________? (do)
Old man: I [5] ________ a postman. I [6] ________ a lot every day. (be, walk)

Language focus extra

Comparatives

1 Complete the table with the comparative forms of the words in the box.

~~comfortable~~ expensive nice interesting safe tall

Add *-r* or *-er*	*more* + adjective
___________	*more comfortable*
___________	___________
___________	___________

2 Complete the sentences with the comparative form of the words in brackets.

1 My house is *smaller than* your house. (small)
2 Jack's room is ___________ Katrina's room. (tidy)
3 Laura's homework is ___________ Abby's homework. (good)
4 This new hotel is ___________ the old hotel. (comfortable)
5 The sofa is ___________ the armchair. (expensive)

Superlatives

3 Write superlative sentences with the words below.

1 The New South China Mall / large / shopping centre / world
The New South China Mall is the largest shopping centre in the world.
2 Vostok in Antarctica / cold / place on Earth
____
3 My bedroom / good / room in the house
____
4 This is / comfortable / chair
____
5 I'm not / bad / student / in our class
____

Comparatives and superlatives

4 Circle the correct form.

1 **A:** I think New York is **more exciting / the most exciting** city in the world!
B: I don't agree. I think that London is **more exciting / the most exciting** than New York.
2 **A:** Buses are **safer / the safest** than trains.
B: I don't agree. I think that trains are **safer / the safest** form of transport.
3 **A:** I think that Tokyo is **more expensive / the most expensive** city in the world.
B: I read that Singapore is **more expensive / the most expensive** than Tokyo.

should/shouldn't

5 Complete the sentences with *should* or *shouldn't* and the verbs in the box.

take go meet phone stay ~~wear~~

1 It's cold today. You *should wear* a warm coat.
2 The train leaves at 10 a.m. We ___________ at 9:45.
3 It's raining. You ___________ your umbrella.
4 It's late. You ___________ to bed now.
5 I've got an exam tomorrow. I ___________ up late.
6 You've got a toothache. You ___________ the dentist.

6 Put the words in the correct order to make questions. Then complete the answers.

1 we / Should / get up / tomorrow / early
A: *Should we get up early tomorrow*?
B: Yes, *we should*.
2 wear / I / to the party / should / What
A: ___________________________?
B: You ___________ your blue dress.
3 use / my calculator / in the exam / Should / I
A: ___________________________?
B: No, ___________
4 we / When / meet / should
A: ___________________________?
B: We ___________ at 9 a.m.
5 Should / book / I / a hotel
A: ___________________________?
B: Yes, ___________
6 What / do / should / this afternoon / I
A: ___________________________?
B: You ___________ your homework.

can, will for making a polite request

7 Complete the sentences with *can* or *will*.

1 ___________ you please finish your homework in time?
2 ___________ I put the sandwiches in the fridge?
3 ___________ I see your ID card, please?
4 ___________ you say thanks to your mum for me?
5 ___________ I ask you something?
6 ___________ you help me find my dog, please?

Language focus extra

UNIT 4

should

1 Two friends are planning a party. Write sentences and questions with *should*. Add extra words if necessary.

1 we / ask your parents for permission?
' *Should we ask your parents for permission?* '
'I asked them yesterday.'
2 we / invite?
' ______________________________ '
'Everyone in the class.'
3 they / bring some food and drink?
' ______________________________ '
'No, my mum is going to get everything.'
4 everyone / arrive / 8 p.m. Is that OK?
' ______________________________ '
'Yes, about 8 p.m. is fine.'
5 I / wear?
' ______________________________ '
'Your blue skirt and white T-shirt.'
6 I / bring some dance music. What do you think?
' ______________________________ '
'Yes, that's a good idea.'

must

2 Complete the sentences with *must* or *mustn't*.

1 You *mustn't* forget to call me tonight.
2 Students ____________ write in pen, not pencil.
3 You ____________ tell anyone. It's a secret.
4 Tell them that they ____________ relax more. It's OK.
5 We ____________ make a lot of noise. This is the library.
6 I ____________ be late, because Dad gets angry.

3 Circle the correct options.

1 You **shouldn't** / **must** be scared to follow your dreams.
2 You **should** / **shouldn't** make promises you can't keep.
3 You're always tired. You really **should** / **mustn't** get more sleep.
4 You **must** / **mustn't** listen more, and speak less.
5 You **must** / **mustn't** criticise other people. It's not nice.
6 You **must** / **shouldn't** wear your glasses. You can't see without them!
7 You **shouldn't** / **must** give up. Try again!
8 You **mustn't** / **shouldn't** drink that water. It'll make you sick.
9 You **must** / **should** do something creative if you're bored.

have to/*don't have to*

4 Complete the sentences and questions with the correct form of *have to*.

1 You *don't have to* phone. You can email for information.
2 At my school, we ____________ play hockey, but there is a school team.
3 Doctors ____________ study for seven or eight years.
4 Why ____________ (she) do the exam again?
5 My brother ____________ study much. He's really clever.
6 ____________ (we) take a sleeping bag with us?
7 I ____________ help around the house, but I don't mind.
8 It's OK. You ____________ speak quietly. The baby woke up a few minutes ago.

5 Complete the sentences with *don't have to* or *mustn't* and the verbs in the box.

have	go	~~use~~	do	play
speak	forget	watch		

1 You *mustn't use* your mobile phone. It's not allowed.
2 You ____________ your homework now. You can do it later.
3 We ____________ a film. We can go out if you like.
4 You ____________ your first aid kit when you go camping.
5 You ____________ a snack now. We're going to have dinner in 10 minutes.
6 We ____________ to school today. It's a holiday.
7 It's OK. You ____________ slowly. I understand you.
8 It's 1 o'clock in the morning. You ____________ your guitar now. Go to sleep!

Language focus extra

will/won't

1 Complete the text with *will* and the words in the box.

be	do	~~go~~	have	study	work

My plans for the future: first, I [1] *will go* to university and I [2] ________ Engineering. I think that Engineering [3] ________ very important because we [4] ________ so many new developments in science and technology. Then I [5] ________ research at a university in Australia. After that, I [6] ________ in a company to make new inventions.

2 Circle the correct words.

Children [1] **will / won't** (circled: won't) go to school because they [2] **will / won't** study at home. We [3] **will / won't** have electric cars because there [4] **will / won't** be enough petrol. People [5] **will / won't** work in factories because robots [6] **will / won't** do all the work.

3 Write questions with *will*. Then write short answers.

1 robots / clean our homes
Will robots clean our homes? Yes, they will. ✓
2 all countries / speak one language
________ ✗
3 aeroplanes / be faster
________ ✓
4 the climate / be warmer
________ ✗
5 people / live longer
________ ✓
6 the world / be more peaceful
________ ✓

4 Complete the sentences with the correct form of *will* or *won't*.

1 I *won't* do my homework now. I'm too tired.
2 I think it ________ rain tomorrow. The sky is clear.
3 I'm sure the teacher ________ give us homework tomorrow. She always does that.
4 We ________ have our Maths class later because our teacher is not here.
5 Josh is a good friend. He ________ tell your secret to anyone.
6 I know that my tablet ________ be here when I come back because it's very safe.

Question tags

5 Match the sentence halves.

1 You've got a new website, *c*
2 We should leave now, ____
3 You have to check your email, ____
4 This course about technology is going to be very interesting, ____
5 He is looking for a job in IT, ____
6 She bought that amazing new computer, ____

a shouldn't we?
b didn't she?
c haven't you?
d isn't he?
e don't you?
f isn't it?

6 Read the situations, then write question tags asking your friend to agree with you. Use the information in brackets.

1 Your computer has broken down and you need a new one. (have to buy)
I have to buy a new computer, don't I? ?
2 Your P.E. class finishes early today. (go home)
____
3 Your friend hasn't checked his email today. (forget to check)
____
4 You must catch your train. (have to leave early)
____
5 Your friend has got a new tablet and you like it very much. (be great)
____
6 A friend of yours, Jessica, has passed her driving test. (get driving license)
____

Language focus extra

be going to

1 Complete the sentences with the correct form of *be going to* and the words in the box.

buy	get	not go	~~study~~	take	work

1 I *am going to study* History at university.
2 Rita ___________ in her dad's shop this summer.
3 My brother ___________ a year out after university.
4 My parents ___________ a new house next year.
5 Sam and Linda ___________ married next year.
6 We ___________ to summer camp this year.

2 Write questions and short answers with *be going to*.

1 What *are you going to do* this summer? (you, do)
2 Where ___________ next year? (Tina, work)
3 When ___________? (your parents, arrive)
4 ___________ this summer? (they, visit Canada)
No, they ___________.
5 ___________ next year? (I, learn to drive)
Yes, I ___________.
6 ___________ Medicine? (your sister, study)
Yes, she ___________.

will vs. *be going to*

3 Decide if each sentence is a plan or a prediction. Circle the correct words.

1 It's raining. You **will** / **are going to** need an umbrella.
2 I think it **will** / **is going to** be difficult to find a job.
3 The concert is sold out. You **won't** / **aren't going to** get tickets.
4 We **will** / **are going to** study Japanese next year.
5 Suzanne **will** / **is going to** work as a scientist.
6 You're an excellent student. I'm sure you **will** / **are going to** pass the test.

4 Complete the sentences with the correct form of *will* or *be going to*.

1 My cousin *is going to get* (get) married next year.
2 Our teacher ___________ (come) to class today. She's busy.
3 I ___________ (study) Maths at university. I love numbers.
4 ___________ (you/watch) the film tonight?
5 We ___________ (play) football later. We've got a lot of homework.
6 What ___________ your friends ___________ (do) when they leave school?

Present continuous for future

5 Write sentences with the words. Use the present continuous.

1 I / cook dinner tonight
I'm cooking dinner tonight.
2 Hillary / look after / her sister tomorrow
____
3 My dad / make / a cake for my birthday
____
4 He / sell / his car next week
____
5 We / play / basketball on Friday
____
6 They / do / the shopping this afternoon
____

6 Read Leila, Danny and Suzanne's plans and complete the table with answers about you. Then use the information to write questions and answers with the present continuous.

	Leila	Danny and Suzanne	You
Tonight	study for a test	eat pizza with their friends	___________
This weekend	visit her grandma	watch a football match	___________

1 What / Leila / do / tonight?
What is Leila doing tonight?
She's *studying for a test*.
2 What / Danny and Suzanne / this weekend?
___________? They ___________.
3 Leila / visit / her auntie / this weekend
___________? ___________.
4 Danny and Suzanne / watch a football match / this weekend ?
___________? ___________.
5 you / study for a test / tonight ?
___________? ___________.
6 you / watch a football match / this weekend?
___________? ___________.

Language focus extra

Present perfect: affirmative and negative

1 Complete the sentences with the present perfect form of the verbs in brackets.

1 Gemma *has broken* her ankle. (break)
2 Kate ________ Colombia. (visit)
3 I ________ octopus. (not eat)
4 My brother ________ a new computer game. (invent)
5 We ________ the latest *Hobbit* film. (not see)
6 My parents ________ me a new bicycle. (buy)
7 They ________ to London twice. (go)
8 Some of my classmates ________ this book. (read)

Spelling: past participles

2 Complete the table with the past participle of each verb.

~~jump~~ slip trip stop study like try

Add *-d* or *-ed*	Remove the last letter and add *-ied*	Double consonant and add *-ed*
1 *jumped*	3 ________	5 ________
2 ________	4 ________	6 ________
		7 ________

Present perfect: irregular verbs

3 Write the past participle of each verb.

1 have *had*
2 fall ________
3 feel ________
4 write ________
5 eat ________
6 see ________
7 begin ________
8 break ________

Present perfect: questions

4 Write questions and short answers with the present perfect.

1 have an accident / you
Have you had an accident ________?
No, I *haven't*.
2 Annie / ever / fall off her bike
________?
Yes, she ________.
3 Tony / break his leg
________?
No, he ________.
4 ever / they / win the lottery
________?
No, they ________.
5 she / burn / her finger
________?
Yes, ________.
6 ever / the dog / bite / you
________?
No, it ________.

Past simple vs. present perfect

5 Circle the correct words.

1 I visited / (have visited) a lot of countries in my life.
2 Sam **broke** / **has broken** his wrist two years ago.
3 Ruth **crashed** / **has crashed** her bike yesterday.
4 I **didn't eat** / **haven't eaten** snails, but I want to try them one day.
5 We **didn't ride** / **haven't ridden** a camel when we were in Egypt.
6 **A:** Do you like skiing?
B: I don't know. I **didn't do** / **haven't done** it before.

6 Complete the story with the correct form of the verbs in brackets.

I [1] *went* (go) ice skating yesterday. I [2] ________ (put on) big socks and the skates and [3] ________ (walk) on to the ice, but of course I [4] ________ (slip). I [5] ________ never ________ (break) my leg, but I [6] ________ (think) I had when I [7] ________ (fall)! Ow! I [8] ________ (stand up) and I [9] ________ (fall) again. This time I [10] ________ (cut) my finger with the skate. I think football is much safer!

Language focus extra

one/ones

1 Circle the correct words.

1 A: Which T-shirt would you like, pink or blue?
B: I'd like the blue **one / ones**, please.

2 A: Which biscuits would you like, chocolate or lemon?
B: I'd like the chocolate **one / ones**, please.

3 A: What kind of ticket do you want?
B: Which **one / ones** is the cheapest?

4 A: I really like those kinds of films.
B: Which **one / ones**?
A: Action films.

5 A: Which restaurant do you like best?
B: The **one / ones** on the corner near the park.

6 A: Do you want the same flowers as last time?
B: No, I'd like different **one / ones**, please.

Indefinite pronouns

2 Choose the correct words.

Edinburgh is an amazing city. [1]**Someone / Something** once said that it's the world capital of festivals. There's always [2]**something / somewhere** to do there. In the summer it has the biggest arts festival in the world. There are thousands of events [3]**everything / everywhere** in the city. The shows in the theatres can be expensive, but many of the open-air [4]**one / ones** are free. In winter, the Scottish New Year party is a three-day festival, another [5]**one / ones** that [6]**nowhere / no one** wants to miss.

3 Complete the sentences with the words in the box.

nothing (x2)	something	nobody	~~anything~~	somewhere	anyone

1 Is there *anything* in this plastic bag?
2 I'd like to go ____________ very warm for my holidays!
3 I'm sorry, but there's ____________ we can do to help you.
4 I don't know ____________ who has a fishing boat.
5 We looked for our friends in the kitchen, but there was ____________ there.
6 Put all your work on this memory stick. It's OK, there's ____________ on it.
7 Can I have ____________ to drink please?

too + adjective

4 Complete the sentences with *too* and the words in the box.

tired	big	~~old~~	late	small	cold	excited

1 Your computer's *too old* to have apps.
2 My desk is ____________ to put all these books on.
3 I'm ____________ to go out. I want to sleep!
4 That's the best news ever! I'm ____________ to speak!
5 It's ____________ to have a shower. It's after midnight.
6 It's ____________ to go to the beach. Let's go shopping instead.
7 This laptop is ____________ to take to school. I need a smaller one.

(*not*) adjective + *enough*

5 Match the sentence halves.

1 The wardrobe wasn't big enough *f*
2 My dad says I'm not old enough ______
3 He's good enough at football ______
4 The paper bag wasn't strong enough ______
5 The snow isn't thick enough ______
6 He's intelligent enough ______

a to play for Chelsea.
b to hold all the shopping.
c to go camping alone.
d to become an astronaut.
e to go skiing.
f to put all her clothes in.

too or *enough*?

6 Choose the correct option.

1 The shelf wasn't **too strong / strong enough** to hold all my books.
2 The memory stick was **too small / small enough** to save all the photos.
3 The dog was **too fast / fast enough** to catch and he ran away.
4 The ball was **too heavy / heavy enough** to throw. I couldn't pick it up.
5 He says he's **too good / not good enough** to play the piano in the concert.
6 I was **too tired / tired enough** to get up so I stayed in bed.
7 I'm **too old / not old enough** to drive.

Notes

Notes

Thanks and acknowledgements

The authors and publishers would like to thank a number of people whose support has proved invaluable during the planning, writing and production process of this course.

We would like to thank Diane Nicholls for researching and writing the Get it right pages.

We would like to thank the following for their contributions: Emma Heyderman for writing the Language focus extra starter page and Andrew Jurascheck and Ruth Cox for editorial work.

We would also like to thank the teams of educational consultants, representatives and managers working for Cambridge University Press in various countries around the world.

The authors and publishers are grateful to the following contributors:

Blooberry: concept design

emc design limited: text design and layouts

QBS Learning: photo selection

Development of this publication has made use of the Cambridge English Corpus (CEC). The CEC is a computer database of contemporary spoken and written English, which currently stands at over one billion words. It includes British English, American English and other varieties of English. It also includes the Cambridge Learner Corpus, developed in collaboration with the University of Cambridge ESOL Examinations. Cambridge University Press has built up the CEC to provide evidence about language use that helps to produce better language teaching materials.

The publishers are grateful to the following for permission to reproduce copyright photographs and material:

p. 5: Dreamstime/91383935; p. 7 (BR): Alamy/©Stockbroker/MBI; p. 10 (BL): Shutterstock Images/Jacek Chabraszewski; p. 11 (B/G): Dreamstime/©Andreykr; p. 13 (BL): Dreamstime/©Waihs; p. 13 (CR): Dreamstime/©Sergey Peterman; p. 14 (TR): Alamy/©Tetra Images; p. 15 (TR): Corbis/Image Source; p. 17 (T): Tomas van Houtryve/VII Photo/Profimedia; p. 18 (L): Shutterstock Images/discpicture; p. 18 (TR): Dreamstime/©Citalliance; p. 23(B/G): Getty Images/Aurora Creative; p. 27 (BR): Shutterstock Images/Bryan Busovicki; p. 29 (TC): REX/Ken McKay; p. 29 (1): Ian West/PA Images/ Profimedia; p. 29 (2): James Manning/PA Images/Profimedia; p. 29 (3): Ken McKay/ITV/Shutterstock Editorial/Profimedia; p. 30 (TL): Dreamstime/©MNStudio; p. 35 (B/G): Thinkstock/locu/ iStock; p. 37 (1): Shutterstock Images/Winston Link; p. 37 (2): Shutterstock Images/fokusgood; p. 37 (3): Alamy/©Martin Wierink; p. 37(4): Margo Harrison/Shutterstock; p. 37 (5): Dreamstime/©Agsolphoto; p. 37 (6): Shutterstock Images/ Baloncici; p. 37 (7): Shutterstock Images/Elena Elisseeva; p. 37 (8): Shutterstock Images/ Venus Angel; p. 37 (9): Shutterstock Images/Sergey Karpov; p. 37 (10): Alamy/©Tyson Ellis/Built Images; p. 37 (11): Shutterstock Images/Simon Bratt; p. 38 (TR): Getty/Bloomberg; p. 39 (2): Shutterstock Images/ Africa Studio; p. 39 (3): Shutterstock Images/Photoseeker; p. 39 (7): Shutterstock Images/Maxal Tamor; p. 39 (8): Shutterstock Images/Mats; p. 41 (TL): Shutterstock Images/Lilly Trott; p. 41 (CL): Dreamstime/©Denis Kelly; p. 41 (BL): Alamy/©Adams Picture Library t/a apl; p. 42 (L): Dreamstime/©Andrew David Periam; p. 42 (BR): Dreamstime/©Nataliya Yakovleva; p. 43 (TR): Alamy/©Image Source; p. 43 (CR): Alamy/©Ian Dagnall; p. 43 (CL): Dreamstime/©Joe Sohm; p. 43 (CL): Dreamstime/©Paop; p. 43 (BL): Shutterstock Images/ Kwiatek7; p. 47 (B/G): Dreamstime/©Vlue; p. 49 (CR): Getty Images/Claudia Dewald; p. 52 (C): Shutterstock Images/ Anchiy; p. 53 (BL): Dreamstime/©Anton Vierietin; p. 53 (C): Alamy/©My Lit'l Eye; p. 54 (BL): Shutterstock Images/ Alexander Raths; p. 57 (TR): Shutterstock Images/Izf; p. 61 (7): Dreamstime/©Razihusin; p. 61 (8): Shutterstock Images/ windu; p. 61 (9): Alamy/©acek Lasa; p. 63 (CR): Alamy/©Dream Pictures/Blend Images; p. 63 (BR): Dreamstime/©Natalia Dobrovolska; p. 65 (CL): Dreamstime/©Paul Freeman; p. 65 (BL): Dreamstime/©Andreistanescu; p. 69 (TL): Corbis/Marc Romanelli/Blend Images; p. 71 (B/G): Dreamstime/©Shannon Fagan; p. 73 (1), (2), (3): Dreamstime/©Starstock; p. 73 (4): Rex features/Masatoshi Okauchi; p. 75 (TR): Superstock/ Minden Pictures; p. 75 (CR): Dreamstime/©Lcodacci; p. 76 (T): Dreamstime/©Oleksandr Prykhodko; p. 77 (TR): Alamy/©Beyond Fotomedia GmbH; p. 77 (CL): Shutterstock Images/Irina Schmidt; p. 78 (T): Corbis/Nancy Ney; p. 83 (B/G): Dreamstime/©Edgar Bullon; p. 86 (TL): Superstock/ChameleonsEye; p. 86 (TR): Corbis/Superstock; p. 86 (BL): Dreamstime/©Famveldman; p. 86 (BR): Alamy/©Colin Hawkins/Cultura Creative; p. 87 (1): Dreamstime/©Ammit; p. 87 (2): Getty/Mike Harrington; p. 87 (3): Shutterstock Images/Vitalii Nesterchuk; p. 87 (4): Shutterstock Images/abaghda; p. 89 (C): Superstock/Minden Pictures; p. 89 (BL): Superstock/Minden Pictures; p. 89 (BC): Dreamstime/©Lori H; p. 90 (TL): Alamy/©PHOVOIR; p. 91 (TL): Shutterstock Images/ kearia; p. 91 (BC): Shutterstock Images/TanjaJovicic; p. 91 (TR): Shutterstock Images/newcorner; p. 95 (B/G): Greg Balfour Evans/Alamy/Alamy/Profimedia; p. 97 (1): Alamy/©Dmitriy Shironosov; p. 97 (2): Alamy/©Chris Ryan/OJO Images Ltd; p. 97 (3): Dreamstime/©Shchipkova Elena; p. 97 (4): Dreamsti me/©Lightfieldstudiosprod; p. 97 (5): Alamy/©DreamPictures/ Blend Images; p. 97 (6): Dreamstime/©Wavebreakmedia Ltd; p. 97 (7): Alamy/©Myrleen Pearson; p. 97 (8): Dreamstime/©Weedezign; p. 97 (9): Alamy/©Pablo Paul; p. 97 (10): Dreamstime/©Martinmark; p. 101 (TL): David Wall/Alamy/Profimedia; p. 101 (C): Dreamstime/©Abubjsm; p. 101 (CL): EQRoy/Alamy/Alamy/Profimedia; p. 101 (B): Dreamstime/©Wirestock; p. 102 (T): Shutterstock Images/ magicinfoto; p. 105 (TL): Shutterstock Images/lornet; p. 113: Dreamstime/Sergey Novikov; p. 115 (BC): Dreamstime/©Jovani Carlo Gorospe; p. 116 (a): Dreamstime/©Kosmos111; p. 116 (b): Shutterstock Images/Africa Studio; p. 116 (c): Shutterstock Images/soloir; p. 116 (d): Shutterstock Images/A and N photography; p. 118 (B): Alamy/©Caroline Commins; p. 123: Dreamstime/©Karenr.

The publishers are grateful to the following illustrators:

David Belmonte p. 51; Alberto de Hoyos: p. 25, 32, 85, 95, 99; Nigel Dobbyn: p. 27; Mark Duffin: p. 8, 61, 63, 80; Jose Rubio: p. 9; David Shephard: p. 8, 92; Andrew Painter p. 50; Tony Wilkins p. 52; Norbert Sipos (Beehive Illustration): p. 25, 39, 62, 75, 80, 87, 88; Bob Lea p. 59; Sean Tiffany: p. 32, 64, 100.